DATE DUE

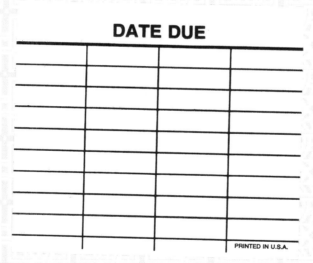

PRINTED IN U.S.A.

STEP·BY·STEP
INDIAN
COOKING

SHARDA GOPAL

with Introductory text by Linda Sonntag

STEP·BY·STEP
INDIAN COOKING

SHARDA GOPAL

with Introductory text by Linda Sonntag

This book is dedicated to my late father and mother, my husband, my daughter Suji and my son Sonny.

PHOTOGRAPHIC CREDITS

8 Carey Mackenzie
9 Michael Freeman
10 Mustafa Sami
11 (above) Mustafa Sami
(left) Douglas Dickens
(below) Michael Freeman
12 (above) Richard Pomeroy
(below) Mustafa Sami
13 Richard Pomeroy

A QUANTUM BOOK

Published by Shooting Star Press, Inc.
230 Fifth Avenue, Suite 1212
New York, NY 10001
USA

This edition printed 1996

ISBN 1-57335-523-2

This book was produced by
Quantum Books Ltd
6 Blundell Street
London N7 9BH

Printed in China by Leefung-Asco Printers Ltd

Contents

The Indian Kitchen

The Recipes

Foreword

More and more people in the West are being introduced to the exotic tastes of Indian food as Indian restaurants mushroom in the streets of nearly every major Western city, and many people have been inspired to try and cook Indian dishes in their own kitchens. Traditionally, however, the knowledge and skills of Indian cooking have been handed down in the family from mother to daughter, and are learned from practical experience. In this way, I learned to cook from my mother. I hope that this book will unravel the mysteries of Indian cooking for those not brought up in the Indian tradition, and make Indian cuisine accessible to even the most amateur cook.

Having been brought up in the Kerala region of southern India, and having lived in both western and northern India, I have been lucky enough to supplement my inherited knowledge with recipes and techniques gleaned from many of the culturally different areas of India. This varied experience and understanding of regional variations has helped me to present this unique collection of recipes. Although the use of spices in the recipes is relatively minimal, it is the subtle combination of these spices and the selection of aromatics that make the dishes in this book different from those that you might find ordinarily in other Indian cookery books or restaurants.

Needless to say, the best Indian food is to be found in Indian homes. All the dishes in this book are those that I serve to my family and friends, and I hope you enjoy making them as much as I have.

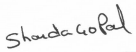

SHARDA GOPAL

INTRODUCTION

India is a land of spectacular contrasts, from the emerald Vale of Kashmir in the snow-clad mountains of the north to the steaming jungles and palm-fringed beaches of the tropical south. Across this vast country of 700 million inhabitants the intricate use of spices unites all the kitchens of the land into producing food that is uniquely Indian.

There are about 25 spices on the shelf in the Indian pantry. Many of them will have come from the back garden along with fresh herbs and bulbs — onions, garlic and shallots. With this huge treasury of flavors the Indian cook can create an infinite number of different dishes. Spices can be used individually or combined, roasted or ground with water into a paste to produce flavors anywhere in the spectrum from sweet to sour, fiery to bland and fragrant to pungent.

Indians are almost intuitively aware of the medicinal properties of the herbs and spices they use to flavor their food, and they eat not just for sheer enjoyment and to stay alive, but to keep their bodies healthy and well-tuned. Apart from their medicinal properties, spices and other condiments can be used to offset the extremes of temperature. In the north, warming spices take the bite out of freezing winter days, and in the south bittersweet tamarind has a soothing effect in the airless midday heat.

ABOVE *Based on Chinese design, this cantilevered fishing net is large enough to catch sufficient fish to feed an entire village with a hearty meal*

ABOVE *The Palm groves of Kerala in southern Indian provide plenty of coconuts, an essential ingredient of many local dishes.*

Of course what is eaten also depends largely on local produce. Broadly speaking, bread is eaten in the north and rice in the south. In the south the food tends to be more fiery (and paradoxically more refreshing, even if it does bring tears to the eyes). In Kerala, in particular, grow the coconut palms, the tamarind and jackfruit trees and the spice gardens that made Cochin rich and famous.

In the south, the tropical heat is put to use to mature pickles and for overnight fermentation of bread and cakes made from ground peas without the addition of yeast. Southerners often steam their food, whereas in the north it is oven-cooked. In Rajasthan in the northwest, picnickers make an impromptu oven by digging a pit for a cow-dung fire on which they will cook spiced meat in a clay pot. The lid of the pot is sealed with dough, and more burning dung is heaped over it. This technique is called *dum* — food is baked slowly all the way through and all the juices are kept in, resulting in the tenderest meat and the richest possible flavor.

In Kashmir the winters are made bearable by cooking with warming spices, particularly cinnamon. People carry around baskets of live charcoal to keep the cold at bay between meals, and these baskets serve a double purpose, often baking an egg or a potato for a hot snack.

Kashmir is a land of lakes and tranquil water gardens. The lakes produce abundant fish and delicious lotus roots. Ingenious farmers make floating vegetable gardens from reeds and mud, which can be towed about or left to drift picturesquely at anchor. When they are harvested, vegetables are sold from boats at the floating market. As autumn draws near there is a frenzy of mushroom picking and all kinds of vegetables, especially chili peppers, are hung up on the rafters to dry to keep the family supplied when the snows come. To see them through the winter, the Kashmiris make a dried spice cake called *ver*, crushing their spices according to a family recipe, then mixing them to a paste with mustard oil. The cake is hung up and bits are broken off it as required.

In the east, the Bengalis are noted for their love of fish and their insatiable desire for sweets, especially jaggery (raw sugar). Sugar cane is pressed to extract the juice, which is then heated over wood fires and patiently stirred for many hours until it is thick enough to set. Lumps of it are eaten as sweets and the Bengalis are so fond of it that they even manage to

FAR LEFT AND LEFT *From the exuberance of the Palace of the Four Winds at Jaipur to the simplicity of the local post office, India is a subcontinent with many architectural delights.*

LEFT AND ABOVE *For most of the time the elephant is a humble beast of burden, earning its keep by carrying and pulling heavy loads, but on festive occasions it is profusely decorated and becomes the center of much attention.*

ABOVE *Nuts are used in both savory and sweet Indian recipes. This nut vendor is a well-known figure outside the Amber Palace in Rajastan.*

RIGHT *Sweets stalls are a common sight on the streets of Indian cities, particularly in western regions. Made from liquid sugar, many varieties are unimaginably sweet to the Western palate.*

ABOVE OPPOSITE *Indians are intuitively aware of the medicinal properties of certain foods, and the medicine man's stall will often display herbs and spices also available from food stalls.*

Indians eat with their hands. The right hand only is used; the left is thought unclean. In some parts of India the whole hand is used, in others just the fingertips. Generally, food is scooped up with a piece of flat bread in the north and mopped up with rice in the south. This means that cleanliness is very important, so hands are washed before and after eating and water for washing is provided even on barrows selling snacks in the streets.

In all parts of India hospitality is legendary. All the dishes, including fruit and sweets, are offered at once. Decoration is simple (nuts, chopped herbs, lemon slices) and sometimes exotic — silver and gold leaf *vark* on special occasions provide a direct, although expensive, source of minerals.

Cold water is drunk with meals. Breakfast, which might be a sweet flaky bread in the foothills of the Himalayas, a potato curry in the capital, Delhi, or a steamed bean cake *(idli)* in the south, is served with tea, sometimes spiced with cinnamon, or with hot strong coffee. During the day an Indian might drink freshly pressed fruit juice (mango is the favorite), coconut milk (in the south), or *lassi*, a sweet and sometimes salty drink made from yogurt. Muslims are forbidden alcohol, but there is plenty of potent liquor available for those who want it. Other drinks include *Asha* (which is distilled from jaggery), palm toddy and, of course, gin.

After a meal the hostess may offer betel leaves — glossy green leaves with mildly anesthetic properties and a refreshing taste. These are chewed and then spat out (or more delicately removed), like gum. They can be taken neat or wrapped around nuts, quicklime, cardamom pods, cloves or tobacco. Shah Jahan, one of India's more colorful rulers and the builder of the Taj Mahal, was even known to wrap them around poison for his less-welcome guests.

Mr and Mrs Gopal, who now live in England, have traveled all over India. From the north they collected enticing meat dishes; from the east, characteristic fish delicacies. The vegetable dishes originate mainly in the south and west. From the south, too, comes their love of coconut, hot spicy vegetable dishes and lentils. This is an individual collection of recipes; the flavor is wholly Indian.

slip it into their vegetable curries.

Bombay in Maharashtra on the west coast, India's Hollywood and boom town founded on seven islands, has its own sweet treats — cookies made of rice flour. They take several days and many processes to make, and are served at religious festivals.

Lucknow in Uttar Pradesh glories in whole chickens stuffed with quails, and a celebration halvah made from the yolks of 100 eggs. Another local extravagance is a pearl pilaf — a dish of rice and "pearls" made by stuffing a chicken's esophagus with a mixture of egg yolks and real gold and silver, and tying it at intervals to resemble a string of pearls. It is then boiled and slit open, and the "pearls" pop out looking very like the real thing.

All over India, the laws of religion rule what is eaten. Hindus are vegetarian, although the priestly caste of Kashmiri Brahmins do eat meat, abstaining instead from cooking with garlic and onions, which they believe inflame the passions. Jains are such strict vegetarians that they will neither eat root vegetables, for fear of killing insects as they dig, nor will they touch tomatoes or eggplants, whose color reminds them of blood. The Muslims will not eat pork and nowhere except in the state of Kerala is it permitted to kill the sacred cow. One sect of Muslims, the Bohris, alternate salt and sweet dishes and begin their meal by eating a pinch of salt in praise of Allah.

Presenting the meal

The traditional way to serve Indian food is on a *thali* or large tray, often of beautifully wrought metal. Each different dish will be in a small metal or earthenware bowl perched around the edge of the tray, or laid out on a low communal brass table. The diners sit on the floor or on very low stools. The carpet is spread with colored cloth to protect it and the guests are given giant colored napkins. The dishes can be wrapped in cotton or silk, which is loosely folded back over the food after it has been served. Often banana leaves will serve as disposable plates. More people today are sitting at a table with chairs, although, in many parts, the men are still served first, and then the women eat together on the floor in the kitchen.

Presentation is an important part of good Indian cooking, and imaginative use of garnishes can make an ordinary dish into something really special. Tomatoes, lettuce and coriander leaves are often used to add color and a crisp texture to savory dishes.

❖

TOP LEFT *Red Peppers Stuffed with Vegetables*, CENTER LEFT *Sardines in a Thick Spicy Sauce*, BELOW LEFT *Baked Fish Stuffed with Mushrooms*, TOP RIGHT *Vegetable Curry, Kerala Style*, CENTER RIGHT *Yellow Rice with Hard-Cooked Eggs*, BELOW RIGHT *Pumpkin Halvah.*

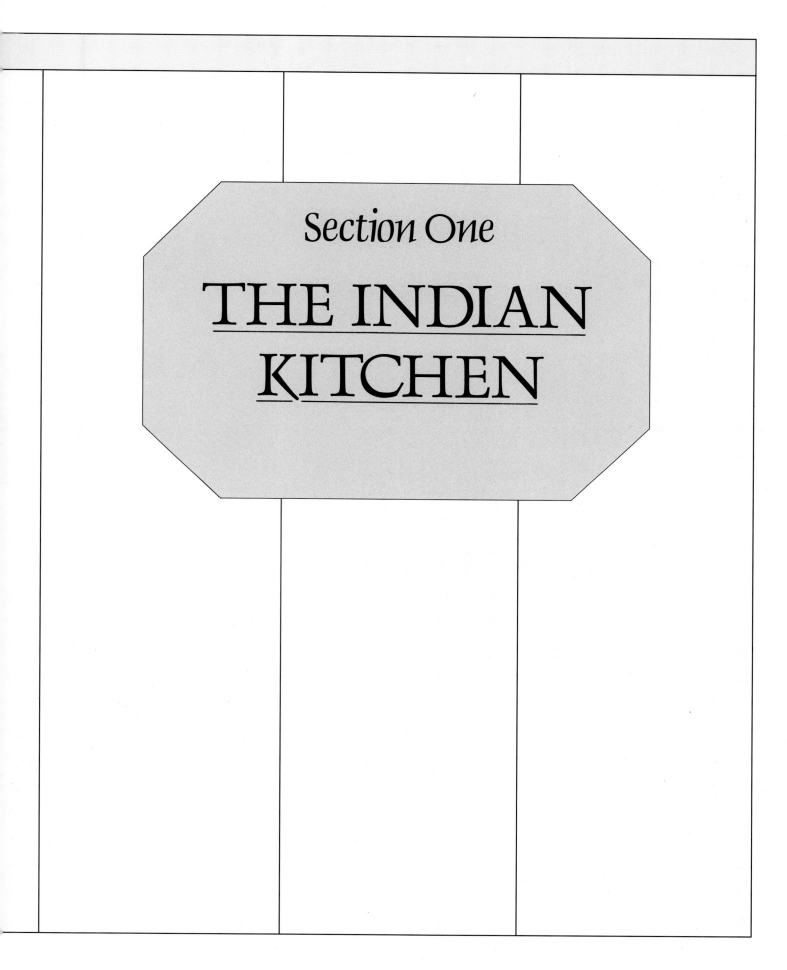

Section One

THE INDIAN KITCHEN

BASIC TECHNIQUES AND TIPS

In India every kitchen was traditionally equipped (and many still are) with a grinding stone — a large flat stone placed on the floor, in front of which the housewife or cook's assistant sat cross-legged, pounding chili peppers and spices with another stone. An electric blender is obviously the modern equivalent of the grinding stone, and can also be used for puréeing chick-peas etc. An electric coffee grinder is ideal for making spice pastes. If you are going to buy a blender or grinder with this purpose in mind, it is best to choose one of the new small food processors, as you will be working with small quantities. A mortar and pestle is still the best bet for very small quantities of hard seeds. Both mortar and pestle should be made of marble, if possible. This will make it quite an expensive item to buy, but remember that metal reacts with acids and wood absorbs flavors.

The old-fashioned way of cooking in India is over a charcoal fire, where food can be spit-roasted or cooked in a heavy pan with hot charcoal heaped on the lid to give an even distribution of heat. The next best thing is a set of cast-iron pans or casseroles that can be used on top of the stove or in the oven, and which have tightly fitting lids. You can improve the fit of a lid by covering the pan with a sheet of aluminum foil and then putting the lid on top. The advantage of cast-iron pans is that they transmit the heat well and stay hot when removed from the stove. Food tends to stick to glazed enamel, so this is best avoided. A set of asbestos mats will give you even better heat control.

For cooking bread, Indians use a heavy flat pan called a tava. Any flat iron pan will be right for this job, and you can use it for roasting spices too.

Other equipment that you need will probably be in your kitchen already. Most essential is a set of good sharp knives for trimming meat and cutting up vegetables. Then you will need a sieve, a colander, a grater with various blades that will tackle anything from a cabbage to a nutmeg, wooden spoons, skewers and a square of cheesecloth.

As there are often a lot of ingredients in a recipe, it is a good idea to measure them out and have them ready before you begin to cook, so that you are not held up looking for things at a crucial moment.

Peeling tomatoes

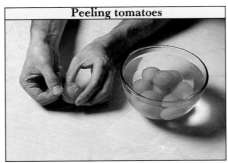

Many of the recipes call for peeled tomatoes. You can use canned tomatoes to save time, and in winter, but fresh, ripe tomatoes are best. Drop them into a bowl of boiling water and leave for a minute or two until a split appears in the skin. Drain and refresh in cold water. The skin can then be removed quite easily.

Adding yogurt

This procedure has to be done carefully or the yogurt will separate. Take the pan from the heat and add the yogurt a spoonful at a time, stirring well between additions. Then return the pan to the heat, stirring all the time, until the sauce bubbles.

Cooking the spice paste until the oil runs clear

The point of this operation is to allow the spices to absorb as much oil as they can, thus releasing their full flavor. When the spices are saturated, the excess oil runs out of them (you can drain it off, if you like), and you can proceed to the next step in the recipe.

Grinding spices

A coffee grinder is ideal for making a spice paste. You can also use a blender, a food processor or a mortar and pestle.

Dropping spices into hot oil

This is often either the first or the last step in an Indian recipe. The oil is heated until very hot and then whole spices or dried chili peppers are dropped into it. Within a few seconds they pop or expand and their concentrated flavor is released. The oil and spices are then used as the starting point of a recipe, or they are poured over the finished dish.

Roasting spices

Heat a flat cast-iron pan without any fat or oil, add the spices and shake them until their roasted fragrance emerges. Roasted spices can be cooled and stored or used immediately, either whole or ground.

Thickening sauces

Flour is not used as a thickening agent in Indian cookery. Instead, spice pastes, yogurt, tomatoes and coconut are all used to thicken and add their own individual flavors.

Clarifying butter to make ghee

You can buy ghee in Indian grocery shops but you can also make it at home. Put some unsalted butter into a heavy saucepan and melt it over a low flame. Let it bubble gently until solid yellow particles form, strain it through cheesecloth and allow to cool. Ghee does not need to be refrigerated.

Browning onions and garlic

This is essential if you want your curry sauces to have a good strong color.

Making yogurt

Yogurt is expensive to buy and if you use it in large quantities it is worth making yourself. Scald 2½ cups milk, then take it off the heat and allow it to cool to lukewarm. Put 2 Tbsp plain yogurt in a bowl, whisk it and then gradually whisk in the milk. Cover the bowl and leave it in a warm place overnight until the yogurt has set. Store in the refrigerator. Keep 2 Tbsp yogurt to make your next batch.

Squeezing tamarind

Break off 2 Tbsp tamarind from the block, and soak it in twice its volume of very hot water for a couple of hours. Now, squeeze the pulp well or press it through a sieve with a wooden spoon to get out all the juice.

Coconuts

You can test the freshness of a coconut by shaking it; if there is plenty of liquid sloshing around inside it, it is fresh. Get the liquid out by punching two holes in the eyes of the coconut. You can drink this liquid (is it very refreshing chilled) but it is not used for cooking in this book. Now give the coconut a good whack with a hammer to open it. Use a knife to pry the flesh from the shell. If this is difficult, put the coconut pieces shell side down over a low flame for a minute or two; the shell will contract and release the flesh. (Alternatively, you can put the coconut in a warm oven for 15 minutes before you crack it.) Peel the brown skin off the white flesh with a potato peeler. Grate the coconut by hand or in a food processor.

If you want to extract the coconut milk for cooking, put the grated coconut in a blender with enough hot water to make it easy for the blades to turn. Strain the mixture through cheesecloth and squeeze out all the liquid. Put the squeezed coconut back in the blender and repeat the process with more hot water. Some recipes call for the milk from the first and second pressings to be used at different stages, so you should, of course, strain them into separate bowls. (The first milk will be much thicker.)

SPICES AND AROMATICS IN THE INDIAN KITCHEN

Spices and aromatics are the very heart of Indian cooking. Flowers, leaves, roots, bark, seeds and bulbs (the simplest of natural ingredients) are used in endless combinations to produce an infinite variety of flavors: sweet, sharp, hot, sour, spicy, aromatic, tart, mild, fragrant or pungent.

The Indian cook aims to create blends of spices so subtle that a completely new taste arises — something indefinable. Sometimes the flavor of one particular spice can be magnified by the careful underplay of several others. As many as 15 spices may be used in one dish, or there might be only one. Spices, unlike herbs, can be used together without loss of flavor.

It is best to buy your spices whole and to grind them at home (see page 18) if the recipe calls for it. Whole spices keep longer than ground ones, which quickly lose their aroma. But even whole spices begin to taste tired after a while, so buy small quantities and keep them in airtight jars in a cool dark place. Do not buy curry powder; this is a blanket term for a blend of inferior spices and will make everything taste the same.

Asafoetida (Hing)
This is a resin that comes from Kashmir. It is bought ground and is said to smell of truffles. The flavor is quite pungent, but it is used mainly for its digestive properties, especially in the cooking of beans, where it combats flatulence. A pinch of it can be fried in hot oil before the rest of the ingredients are cooked.

Biriyani masala
This is a special sweet spice mix for biriyani dishes. Grind together the seeds from 8 cardamom pods, 1oz cinnamon stick, 6 cloves and 1 tsp fennel seeds.

Cardamom (Elaichi)
Pale green cardamom pods contain tiny black seeds and grow in the rain forests of southern India. They have a sweet, fragrant flavor and can be used whole or the seeds can be taken out of the pods and used separately. This is a tedious job, but seeds are not usually sold out of their pods because they lose their flavor too fast. Some recipes use ground cardamom seeds; since are so small, it is best to grind them with a mortar and pestle.

Cayenne pepper (Pisi hui lal mirch)
Cayenne pepper, like paprika, comes from the seeds of plants in the capsicum family. It is a blend of various types of chili powder. The capsicum family is large, ranging from the sweet pepper to the chili pepper. In general, the smaller the fruit, the hotter it is. Cayenne is sold as a powder. It should not be as hot as chili powder, but it is pretty hot and should therefore be used with care.

Chili (Mirchi)
Chili is the hottest flavor on earth. Chili peppers and chili powder should be used with extreme care. Do not take a bite or even lick one to see how its tastes as the effect will be quite devastating. Also, do not touch your mouth or eyes while handling chili peppers — the burning will be intense. Whole chili peppers can be seeded to make them a little less hot. Regulate the quantity of chili recommended in the recipes according to how much you can bear, and do not forget to tell your guests if you have left a whole chili lurking in the curry.

You can now buy fresh green chili peppers at many grocery stores and supermarkets. If you live a long way from a regular supplier of chili peppers, buy them when you see them, wash them, dry them, put them in a jar and fill it to the brim with oil. Screw the lid on tightly and keep them in a cool dark place. This is a very good way of storing them, and you get a flavored oil out of it too. Otherwise chili peppers become moldy quite quickly. If one is moldy, all the others will be infected too and the entire batch should be thrown away.

Chili peppers become red as they ripen, so dried ones are always red. They are dropped into hot oil to release their aroma before other ingredients are added

Chili powder is very hot indeed because it is made from the crushed seeds of the chili, its hottest part. A blend of chili, garlic, cumin and oregano is also sold as chili powder and should not be confused with the chili powder called for in this book.

Cinnamon (Dalchini)
Cinnamon has a rich, warm flavor. It is available as a powder but is much better bought in sticks. You can then break off a piece and add it to the curry. It should be discarded before serving. A lot of cinnamon is grown in Sri Lanka; it is the inner bark of a tree related to the laurel. The outer bark is scraped off and the inner bark peeled off in strips and rolled into sticks, which are then dried.

Cloves (Luong)
Cloves are the flower buds of an evergreen of the myrtle family. They have been used in India for thousands of years, not only in cookery, but to sweeten the breath and to relieve the pain of toothache. They contain a mild anesthetic. Cloves are best bought whole and ground, if necessary, at home with a mortar and pestle. Whole cloves are not eaten, but left on the side of the plate.

Coconut (Nariel)
Fresh coconut may be grated and frozen. You can buy dried unsweetened coconut in packets in Indian groceries or health food stores, and this can be used if the fresh variety is not available. (For how to prepare a coconut, see page 19.)

Coriander (Daniya)
The English name for this spice comes for the Greek koros, meaning "bug". They are small ridged seeds, light brown in color and can be easily squashed under the thumb. They are used powdered or whole.

Fresh green coriander also known as Chinese parsley or cilantro (Hari daniya)
The leaves of the coriander plant are rather like those of flat-leaved parsley, but darker and more brilliant. Fresh coriander is just as easily grown as parsley. The leaves have a very distinctive bittersweet taste. The best way of keeping this herb is in a jug of water in the refrigerator. Tired leaves can be revived by immersing in cold water for an hour, but do not keep them in water as they will become slimy.

Cumin (Jeera)
Cumin seeds are long and slim, similar to caraway seeds, but have a distinctive warm aroma. They are used either whole

or ground, and can be bought ground. However, is it best to buy them whole and grind your own at home, as the ground spice loses its flavor quite quickly. Cumin is often used roasted. Drop the whole seeds into a hot dry pan and cook until the roasted fragrance emerges. Shake the pan to prevent sticking. The seeds can be stored whole, or ground in a coffee grinder and stored or used immediately.

Curry leaves (Kari pulia or Neem)
These are small greenish-gray leaves, a bit like bay, and are grown in many Indian gardens. They can be used fresh or dried; the dried ones can be crumbled onto food, and their aroma is released by its heat and moisture. They are sometimes fried in the oil the food is cooked in, and then discarded. They can also be eaten.

Food colorings
Turmeric and saffron will color food yellow, but you can also buy a vegetable coloring that has no taste. Red food coloring is used on tandoori chicken.

Fennel (Soonf)
Small oval seeds, greenish and with a licorice flavor, they have digestive properties, and are sometimes served roasted at the end of an Indian meal. Used sparingly, they give warmth and sweetness to curries.

Fenugreek (Methi)
These tawny-colored seeds are chunky and very hard. Their bitter taste and aroma are released only by cooking. In powdered form, fenugreek is one of the main ingredients of curry powders; it is also used sparingly on its own. The leaves of the plant, which is related to spinach, are used in India as an herb.

Garam masala
Garam masala, meaning "hot spices", is a mixture of ground spices that is used sparingly, sprinkled either on a finished dish or onto the food just before it has finished cooking. It is far better to grind your own spices than to buy the mixture ready-ground. Purchased garam masala often contains inferior-quality spices and will not keep its flavor for long.

For homemade garam masala, grind together the seeds from 10 cardamom pods, 1oz cinnamon stick, 6 cloves and 6-

8 whole black peppercorns. Store in an airtight jar in a cool place.

Ghee
This is clarified butter and can be made at home (see page 19). The advantage of using ghee is that it can be heated to a very high temperature without burning, and so it is useful for browning onions in order to give a sauce a good rich color, and for sizzling spices before the main ingredients are added to the pan. Because the milk solids have been removed from ghee, it will keep will without being refrigerated. Many people prefer to use unsaturated fats and oils instead of ghee or butter.

Ginger
You can buy ginger ground (soondth) or fresh (adrak). The ground type is the same as that used in baking. The fresh "root" ginger is actually a rhizome, and is fawn in color and knobby. Inside, the ginger is hard, yellow and fibrous; it is easiest to cook with if peeled and grated. You can also chop it if you are going to purée it with other ingredients. Fresh ginger can be kept wrapped in foil in the freezer or in a pot of sandy soil, kept fairly dry. It has quite a hot, pungent flavor and should be used sparingly.

Mango powder (Amchur)
Unripe mangoes are sliced and dried, then powdered and sold as amchur. Amchur has a tart taste. If you are unable to find it, use a dash of lemon or lime juice instead.

Mustard seeds (Rai)
There are both white and black mustard seeds; the black containing a higher proportion of the volatile mustard oil. When dropped into hot oil, the mustard seeds pop, releasing their flavor. (It is best to put a lid over the pan while you do this, or they will fly all over the kitchen.) You can use this technique when shallow-frying Western food to add extra aroma.

Nutmeg and mace (Jaiphal and Javitri)
Mace is the fleshy lattice-like covering of the nutmeg, which is golden brown in color. It is sold whole or powdered. Nutmegs are best bought whole and freshly grated at home.

Oil
Mustard oil, derived from the seeds of the mustard plant, is very popular with south Indian cooks, especially for pickling. This and coconut oil can be bought at Indian groceries. Coconut oil is stirred together with a little warm water to release its aroma before use.

Peanut oil is suitable for Indian cooking, as is the oil labeled simply "vegetable oil".

Paprika
Paprika is the ground seeds from the capsicum or sweet pepper. It is milder than chili powder or cayenne.

Peppercorns (Mirchi)
Peppercorns grow on large bushes in Malabar, on the west coast of India. They are picked by hand just before ripening when they are still green, then left in the sun to dry and become black and crinkly. White peppercorns are the mature fruit, left to ripen on the bush, with the outer husk removed. This is traditionally done by immersing sacks of peppercorns in running streams. Bacteria get to work and loosen the husks and the water finishes the job. The peppercorns are then trodden in vats, like grapes, to rid them of the final traces of husk.

Black pepper is more aromatic; white pepper is stronger and hotter. Black pepper should always be bought whole and freshly ground over your food as it loses its aroma fast.

Poppy seeds (Khus-khus)
It is the milky juice in the poppy's seed pod from which opium is derived — the seeds themselves have no narcotic properties. They are small, black and hard. There is also a white type.

Saffron (Zaffran)
Saffron is the most expensive spice of all. It is the filaments from a specially cultivated crocus — 75,000 stamens are needed to make 4oz of the spice. It is grown in Kashmir and used on festive occasions to give food a bright yellow color and a distinctive aroma. The filaments can be lightly roasted, crumbled in a little hot water and left to infuse to bring out their full strength. Buy saffron only from a reputable spice

dealer or you may get an adulterated product, or something that is not saffron at all, especially if you buy it ready-powdered.

Sambar powder

This is a delicious aromatic spice mix used in a number of recipes in this book.

½ cup coriander seeds
1 tsp asafoetida
4 whole red chili peppers
6 curry leaves
2 Tbsp polished split black lentils
  (urid dal)
2 Tbsp chana dal
2 Tbsp fenugreek seeds
1 Tbsp mustard seeds
4-6 whole black peppercorns

Roast together the first four ingredients and set them aside. Then roast each of the remaining ingredients separately. Some take very little roasting before the fragrance emerges and would burn if roasted with the rest. Now grind all the roasted spices together to a fine powder and store in a screw-topped jar.

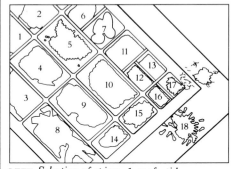

LEFT *Selection of spices. 1 asafoetida,*
2 garam masala, 3 turmeric, 4 ground
cinnamon, 5 black peppercorns,
6 poppy seeds, 7 nutmeg, 8 cassia,
9 ground ginger, 10 crushed red chili
peppers, 11 fenugreek, 12 cumin,
13 black mustard seeds, 14 paprika,
15 cardamom, 16 mustard seeds,
17 saffron, 18 cloves.

Tamarind (Amli)

A tamarind looks a little like a cinnamon-colored pod of broad beans. Tamarind grows on tall trees and is peeled and seeded when ripe. The fruit is then squashed into bricks and this is how you buy it. It has a very tart citric flavor; if you cannot find it, use a dash of lemon or lime juice instead. (For preparing tamarind juice, see page 19.)

Turmeric (Huldi)

Turmeric is a rhizome related to ginger. Bought as a powder, it gives curries their characteristic golden yellow color. It has a delicate taste and is mildly antiseptic, although it becomes bitter if too much is used. Indians often use turmeric with beans because of its digestive properties.

Vindaloo paste

This is a very hot, spicy paste. Chili peppers may be used with their seeds if you like particularly fiery food. In western India the Christians eat pork vindaloo. For those not permitted pork, vindaloo goes well with beef, lamb or shrimp.

10 red chili peppers
4 Tbsp finely grated fresh ginger
12 cloves garlic, 4 chopped and 8 thinly sliced
½ tsp fenugreek seeds
1 tsp mustard seeds
1 tsp cumin seeds
3 Tbsp white wine vinegar
6 Tbsp oil
2 cups chopped onion
1lb tomatoes, peeled
seeds from 8 cardamom pods

Grind or pound the chili peppers, half of the ginger, chopped garlic, fenugreek, mustard and cumin, and mix them to a paste with the vinegar. Do not add any water. Heat the oil and fry the onion until golden, then add the tomatoes and squash them into a paste as you cook. Stir in the spicy vinegar paste you have already made, add the remaining spices and fry until the oil runs out of them. The paste is then ready. Allow it to cool and store in an airtight container in a cool, dark place.

Typical Menus

A perfectly balanced Indian meal will have dishes that cover a whole range of flavors from mild to hot and from sweet to sour. Texture, too, is considered. There will be dishes that are crunchy, soft, dry, moist, rough and smooth. Some will be served piping hot, while others may be chilled. There might be a meat dish (in the meat-eating households of the north), a fish dish, lentils, rice, two or three vegetable dishes and a salad, several chutneys and a cooling yogurt. The following are suggestions for menus using recipes from this book, although obviously a meal need not contain more than two or three complementary dishes.

 ## SPICY MENU

Dal Curry 1 (see page 28)

Green Beans Toran 1 (see page 56)

Cauliflower with Potatoes and Tomatoes (see page 69)

Meat Curry with Yogurt (see page 81)

Shrimp Vindaloo (see page 117)

Wholewheat Unleavened Bread (see page 128)

Green Mango Chutney (see page 140)

Beet Halvah (see page 149)

Shrimp Vindaloo is a hot and spicy curry, and this menu would be ideal for those particularly partial to hot dishes. Dal Curry is very nourishing and full of protein, and served in conjunction with dry Green Beans Toran it beautifully balances the different and exciting tastes of this meal. Potato and bread provide starch, and can be used to mop up the rich and varied sauces of the other dishes. For those who might find the Vindaloo a little hot on its own, Green Mango Chutney can be deliciously sweet and soothing. Finally, the Beet Halvah is an excellent last course, providing coolness and sweetness.

CELEBRATION MENU

Chick-peas with Mango and Coconut (see page 36)

Extra Thick Buttermilk Curry (see page 40)

Lemon Rice (see page 132)

Whole Roast Chicken (see page 105)

Stuffed Okra (see page 61)

Tamarind Chutney (see page 137)

Pineapple Pudding (see page 148)

This is a celebration meal centered around the Whole Roast Chicken, with delicately fragrant Lemon Rice and spicy Stuffed Okra as the main accompaniments. Although this menu would suit those who prefer milder Indian cooking, it nevertheless provides a variety of contrasting and complementary tastes and textures. The Chick-peas with Mango and Coconut is crunchy and blends well with the Buttermilk Curry (a popular Gujarati dish) and the chicken in terms of texture and heat, whereas a good tangy flavor is provided by the chunky Tamarind Chutney.

SAVORY MENU

Yogurt Bread (see page 128)
Coconut Chutney (see page 136)
Peanut Soya Sauce (see page 140)
Fried Spiced Meat Keema (see page 85)
Carrot Toran (see page 73)

Yellow Rice with Hard-Cooked Eggs (see page 120)
Melon with Orange Juice (see page 145)

The Punjabis make full use of carrots when they are in season, using them in sweet as well as savory dishes. In this menu Carrot Toran is a dry spicy dish that not only complements the main dish of Fried Spiced Meat Keema but also adds color to this tasty spread of Indian cooking.

MEAT & FISH MENU

Green Lentil and Banana Curry (see page 37)
Potato Masala Curry (see page 52)
Mashed Eggplant (see page 60)
Meatball and Cauliflower Curry (see page 89)
Fish Curry with Yogurt (see page 113)

Vegetable Biriyani (see page 77)
Black Lentil Chutney (see page 141)
Mango Soufflé (see page 149)

Both meat and fish are essential ingredients of this menu and, together with the Vegetable Biriyani, provide a substantial meal. The smooth texture of the Mashed Eggplant effectively offsets the spice and "bite" of the Potato Masala Curry, and it is a soothing dish. Mango Soufflé is both light and fluffy in texture, and is an easily digested conclusion to this satisfying meal.

VEGETARIAN MENU 1

Bitter Melon with Onion Stuffing (see page 65)
Cauliflower with Coconut Milk (see page 68)
Fried Spiced Shrimp (see page 117)
Yellow Rice with Hard-Cooked Eggs (see page 120)
Tomato Salad (see page 144)

Curried Pumpkin and Black-eyed Peas (see page 32)
Steamed Plantain Cake (see page 153)

This is a menu for non-meat eaters; the peas, shrimp and eggs provide plenty of protein. The Bitter Melon with Onion Stuffing is, as its name suggests, a bitter dish and is included for those interested in the more unusual tastes of Indian cooking. In Bengal melons are served first so that the bitterness cleans the palate in preparation for the main dishes. As this meal is fairly mild, Steamed Plantain Cake is an ideal hot pudding to end the meal.

VEGETARIAN MENU 2

Dal Bread (see page 129)
Vegetable Curry with Roasted Coconut (see page 45)
Green Coriander Chutney (see page 137)
Dry Spiced Potato (see page 49)
Vegetable Curry, Kerala Style (see page 48)

Vegetable Biriyani (see page 77)
Plantain Jaggery (see page 153)

Vegetarians in India rarely eat eggs and get their protein from other ingredients, such as nuts. This menu is for strict vegetarians, containing an enticing assortment of vegetable dishes including one with a rich sauce (Vegetable Curry with Roasted Coconut), one cooked dry (Dry Spiced Potato) and one cooked with rice (Vegetable Biriyani).

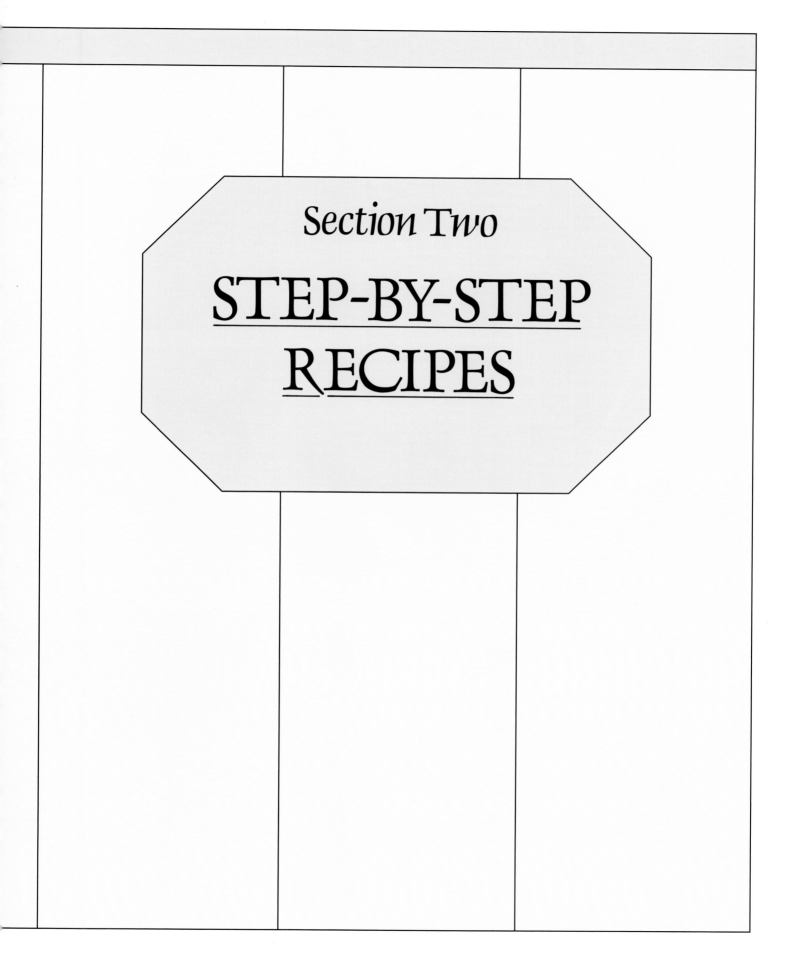

Section Two

STEP-BY-STEP
RECIPES

LEGUMES
Dal

India has over 60 varieties of legumes, which provide a primary source of protein for her millions of vegetarians. When cooked, legumes can be left whole or puréed, making them extremely versatile as ingredients for curries, stuffings and patties. They can even be roasted or deep-fried for garnishes or snacks.

To cook legumes, first pick them over and remove any foreign matter. The larger varieties should be soaked overnight (at least 10 hours). If you are in a hurry, you can bring them to a boil, continue boiling for a couple of minutes and then take the pan off the heat and leave it to stand for an hour before cooking.

Soaked beans are best rinsed to get rid of some of the starch. They will then need to simmer for anything from 15 minutes to over an hour, depending on size and age. Simmer them with the lid slightly open to let the steam escape.

Sometimes beans are simmered with a few of the aromatics that will be used in the curry, but most of them are added at a later stage because of the lengthy cooking time. Ginger and turmeric are favorite flavorings for beans and asafoetida is often added to combat flatulence.

Sprouted legumes are even more nutritious than non-sprouted ones. Sprouted lentils can be purchased in some supermarkets and health food shops, but they are expensive. It is cheap and easy to sprout your own lentils at home. Spread them out in a shallow dish and sprinkle them with water or spray them with a plant sprayer. As soon as the water has been absorbed (after an hour or two), spray them again. Keep them moist for two or three days, and once they have sprouted, they will be ready to eat.

DAL CURRY I

INGREDIENTS (Serves 2)
¾ cup toor dal
2 Tbsp oil
½ tsp mustard seeds
½ tsp cumin seeds
1 small onion, finely chopped
leaves from 1-2 sprigs coriander
2 tomatoes, peeled and chopped
½ tsp turmeric
1 clove garlic, finely chopped
2 green chili peppers, sliced
salt

1 Pick over the dal and wash it well. Bring 3¾ cups water to a boil, add the dal and simmer for about 15 minutes, until you can crush the dal with the back of a wooden spoon. Set aside, covered.

2 Heat the oil in a skillet and add the mustard seeds. Sizzle for a few seconds until all the seeds have popped.

3 Add the cumin seeds, onion and half the coriander leaves and fry, stirring, until the onion is golden.

4 Add the tomato, turmeric, garlic and chili, stirring well and mashing the tomato with the spices to make a paste.

5 Add the dal with a little of its cooking water. Stir well, heat through and add salt to taste. Garnish with the remaining coriander leaves.

DAL CURRY II

INGREDIENTS (Serves 4)
1½ cups toor dal
¼ cup butter or ghee
½ tsp cumin seeds
1½ Tbsp chick-pea flour or besan flour
salt
leaves from 1 sprig of coriander, finely chopped
1-2 green chili peppers, chopped

1 Pick over the dal and wash it well. Bring about 5 cups water to a boil, add the dal and simmer for 10-15 minutes until soft. Strain off excess water and mash the dal well or purée in a blender or food processor. Set aside.

2 Heat the butter or ghee in a pan and when hot, fry the cumin seeds for a few seconds until their flavor emerges. Add to the dal.

3 In a small bowl, mix the chick-pea flour with 3 Tbsp water until it forms a smooth paste.

4 Stir the paste into the dal and simmer over low heat, stirring occasionally, for about 5 minutes, until it is thick and soupy.

5 Stir in salt to taste and garnish with coriander leaves and green chili.

(Photograph, see page 30)

DAL AND COCONUT CURRY
(Dal Nariel)

INGREDIENTS (Serves 2)
¾ cup toor dal
1½ tsp turmeric
1½ tsp chili powder
1 small onion, finely chopped
2-3 Tbsp grated fresh coconut
1 tomato, peeled and chopped
2 Tbsp oil
1tsp mustard seeds
4-6 curry leaves
salt

1 Pick over the dal and wash it well. Bring about 3¾ cups water to a boil, add the dal and simmer for 10-15 minutes, until soft and mushy.

2 Stir in the turmeric and chili powder, cover and keep hot over low heat.

3 Put half the onion with the coconut in a blender or food processor, add 1 Tbsp water and blend until smooth. Stir into the dal with the tomato.

4 Heat the oil in a pan and add the mustard seeds. When all the seeds have popped, add the remaining onion and fry until golden. Add to the dal.

5 Stir in the curry leaves and salt to taste.

DAL AND MUSHROOM CURRY
(Kumban Dal)

INGREDIENTS (Serves 4)
1 cup red split lentils (masoor dal)
1½ tsp turmeric
1½-2 cups button mushrooms, halved
1 Tbsp finely grated fresh ginger
1 green chili pepper, sliced
2 cups chopped onion
1 Tbsp sambar powder
2 Tbsp grated fresh or dried unsweetened coconut
1 cup peeled and chopped tomatoes
2 Tbsp oil
1 tsp mustard seeds
4-6 curry leaves
salt

1 Pick over the dal and wash it thoroughly. Cook in about 5 cups water with the turmeric, for 10-15 minutes, until it can be crushed with the back of a wooden spoon.

2 Add the mushrooms, ginger, chili and half of the onion, and cook for 10 minutes longer.

3 Meanwhile, blend the sambar powder with the coconut in a blender or food processor, add to the curry with the tomato and cook for a further 6-8 minutes, until the sauce is thick and smooth.

4 Heat the oil in a pan, add the mustard seeds and let them sizzle for a few seconds until they have all popped.

5 Add the curry leaves and remaining onion and fry until the onion is golden. Add to the curry with salt to taste.

(Photograph, see page 31)

ABOVE Dal Curry II
See page 28

ABOVE Dal and Mushroom Curry
(Kumban Dal)
See page 29

CURRIED PUMPKIN AND BLACK-EYED PEAS
(Pethi Lobhia)

INGREDIENTS (Serves 4)
1 cup dried black-eyed peas, soaked
* overnight*
8oz unripe red pumpkin* or butternut squash,
* peeled and thinly sliced*
2 green chili peppers, cut into 4 pieces
2 Tbsp coconut oil
4 curry leaves
salt
*sold as calabaza *in Latin American*
grocery stores.

1 Drain the peas and cook in fresh water for about 10 minutes, until barely tender.

2 Add the pumpkin and green chili and cook for a further 5-7 minutes, until tender.

3 Mix the coconut oil with 1 Tbsp water to release its aroma, then add to the curry with the curry leaves and salt to taste.

(Photograph, see page 34)

SPLIT PEA AND YAM CURRY
(Koot)

INGREDIENTS (Serves 4)
1 cup yellow split peas (chana dal)
½ tsp turmeric
½ tsp chili powder
1lb yams, peeled and cubed
8oz white pumpkin (see page 40) or green
* plantain, peeled and cubed*
1⅓-2 cups grated fresh or dried unsweetened
* coconut*
1 tsp cumin seeds
1 tsp mustard seeds
2-3 Tbsp oil
1 red chili pepper, cut into pieces
6-8 curry leaves
salt

1 Soak the split peas in water with the turmeric and chili powder for about 2 hours. Drain and cook in about 5 cups water for 15-20 minutes, until the peas can be crushed with the back of a wooden spoon and most of the water has evaporated.

2 Cook the yam and pumpkin or plantain in water to cover for about 15 minutes, until tender but not soft.

3 Add the cooked peas to the vegetables over low heat, stirring occasionally.

4 Blend three-quarters of the coconut with the cumin seeds in a blender or food processor for a few seconds only, and add to the curry.

5 Fry the mustard seeds in the oil until they have all popped. Add the red chili, curry leaves and remaining coconut. Fry for a further 3-4 minutes, stirring, then add to the curry.

6 Take the curry off the heat, cover and let stand for 3-4 minutes, then add salt to taste.

(Photograph, see page 35)

CHICK-PEAS TORAN
(Chana Toran)

INGREDIENTS (Serves 4)
scant 1 cup chick-peas
5 Tbsp oil
1 onion, finely chopped
2 cloves garlic, finely chopped
1 Tbsp finely grated fresh ginger
2 green chili peppers, thinly sliced
leaves from 1 sprig of coriander, finely chopped
salt
½ tsp ground cumin
1 cup sliced tomatoes
⅔ cup grated fresh coconut

1. Pick over the chick-peas, wash thoroughly and soak for at least 10 hours in water. Drain and cook in fresh water for 1-1½ hours, depending on the age of the chick-peas, until tender but not soft.

2. Heat the oil in a pan, add the onion and fry until golden.

3. Add the garlic, ginger, green chili and half the coriander leaves, stir and fry for 3-4 minutes, then drain the chick-peas and stir these in with salt to taste.

4. Heat a small pan without fat or oil, add the ground cumin and cook for 1-2 minutes until the fragrance emerges. Sprinkle over the curry.

5. Garnish with the remaining coriander leaves, the sliced tomatoes and grated coconut.

SPICED CHICK-PEAS
(*Masala Chana*)

INGREDIENTS (Serves 4)
scant 1 cup chick-peas
½ cup butter or ghee
1 onion, finely chopped
2 cloves garlic, finely chopped
1 Tbsp finely grated fresh ginger
1 cup peeled and chopped tomatoes
½ tsp ground coriander
½ tsp chili powder
1 Tbsp mango powder (amchur)
½ tsp ground cumin
1 tsp garam masala
leaves from 1 sprig of coriander
salt

1. Pick over the chick-peas, wash thoroughly and soak in water for at least 10 hours. Drain and cook in fresh water for 1-1½ hours, depending on the age of the chick-peas, until tender but not soft.

2. Heat the butter or ghee in a pan, add the onion, garlic and ginger and fry until the onion is golden.

3. Add the tomato, ground coriander, chili, mango powder, cumin, garam masala and half of the coriander leaves. Cook, stirring briskly to mash the tomato with the back of the spoon into a paste.

4. Drain the chick-peas, reserving the cooking liquor, and add to the pan with 2 Tbsp of the liquor. Cover and cook over low heat, stirring occasionally, for about 10 minutes, until the chick-peas have absorbed the flavors of the spices.

5. Sprinkle on the remaining coriander leaves and add salt to taste.

(Photograph, see page 38)

CURRIED CHICK-PEAS
(*Chana Curry*)

INGREDIENTS (Serves 4)
scant 1 cup chick-peas
4-5 Tbsp butter or ghee
1 tsp mustard seeds
1 onion, finely chopped
1 Tbsp finely grated fresh ginger
1 green chili, chopped
4-6 curry leaves
⅔-1 cup grated fresh coconut
salt

1. Pick over the chick-peas, wash thoroughly and soak in water for at least 10 hours. Cook in fresh water for 1-1½ hours, depending on the age of the chick-peas, until tender but not soft.

2. Heat the butter or ghee in a pan and add the mustard seeds. Let them sizzle for a few seconds until they have all popped.

3. Add the onion and fry until golden.

4. Drain the chick-peas, reserving the cooking liquor. Add the chick-peas to the pan with the ginger, green chili and about 2 Tbsp cooking liquor. Cover and cook over low heat, stirring occasionally, for 10 minutes, until the chick-peas have absorbed the flavors of the sauce.

5. Stir in the curry leaves and grated coconut and add salt to taste.

ABOVE Split Pea and Yam Curry
(Koot)
See page 32

OPPOSITE Curried Pumpkin and
Black-eyed Peas
(Pethi Lobhia)
See page 32

SPECIAL CURRIED CHICK-PEAS
(Chana Curry)

INGREDIENTS (Serves 4)
scant 1 cup chick-peas
½ tsp baking soda
½ cup butter or ghee
1 onion
2 or 3 bay leaves
seeds from 1 cardamom pod
1 inch cinnamon stick
3 cloves
1 Tbsp finely grated fresh ginger
1 tsp fennel seeds
3 cloves garlic, chopped
¾ cup peeled and chopped tomatoes
1 tsp chili powder
1½ tsp ground cumin
leaves from 1-2 sprigs coriander
½ tsp paprika
2 tsp ground coriander
1 Tbsp lemon juice
salt

1 Pick over the chick-peas and wash thoroughly. Soak in water for at least 10 hours. Drain and cook in 5 cups fresh water with the baking soda for 1-1½ hours, depending on the age of the chick-peas, until tender but not soft.

2 Heat three-quarters of the butter or ghee in a good-sized pan and add the onion, bay leaves, cardamom seeds, cinnamon, cloves, ginger, fennel seeds, garlic and tomatoes. Fry until the onion is golden, mashing the tomato with the back of a wooden spoon to make a thick paste.

3 Add the chili powder, half the cumin, the coriander leaves and paprika and cook for 3-4 minutes, stirring occasionally.

4 Add the cooked chick-peas with about ⅔ cup of their cooking liquor and cook over low heat for 8-10 minutes.

5 In a separate pan, heat the remaining butter or ghee and, when hot, add the remaining ground cumin. Fry for a few seconds, until the fragrance emerges, and add to the chick-peas.

6 Sprinkle on the ground coriander and lemon juice, and add salt to taste.

CHICK-PEAS WITH MANGO AND COCONUT
(Aam aur Nariel Ke Chana)

INGREDIENTS (Serves 2)
scant ½ cup chick-peas
flesh of ½ coconut
8oz green mango, peeled
2 Tbsp butter or ghee
½ tsp ground cumin
salt

1 Pick over the chick-peas, wash thoroughly and soak in water for at least 10 hours. Drain. Cook in fresh water for 1-1½ hours, depending on the age of the chick-peas, until tender but not soft.

2 Chop the coconut flesh and mango into small even pieces and mix with the chick-peas. Heat through in a skillet for 3-4 minutes, stirring briskly.

3 In a separate pan, heat the butter or ghee and fry the cumin for a few seconds until the fragrance emerges. Add to the vegetables. Add salt to taste.

(Photograph, see page 39)

GREEN LENTIL CURRY
(Moong Curry)

INGREDIENTS (Serves 2)
¾ cup whole green lentils (moong dal)
½ cup butter or ghee
1 onion, finely chopped
1 green chili pepper, chopped
2 cloves garlic, chopped
1 Tbsp finely grated fresh ginger
½ cup peeled and chopped tomatoes
½ tsp turmeric
½ tsp chili powder
leaves from 1 sprig of coriander
1 tsp cumin seeds
salt

1 Pick over the lentils, wash thoroughly and soak in water for about 4 hours. Drain and cook in fresh water to cover for about 30 minutes, until tender.

2 Meanwhile, heat three-quarters of the butter or ghee in a pan, add the onion, green chili, garlic and ginger and fry until the onion is golden.

3 Add the tomato and cook, mashing it with the back of a wooden spoon to make a paste.

4 Add the turmeric, chili powder and coriander leaves and continue to cook until the fat runs clear of the spices.

5 Add the lentils and about 2 Tbsp of their cooking liquor and cook for a further 5 minutes.

6 Meanwhile, fry the cumin seeds in the remaining butter or ghee for a few seconds, until the fragrance emerges, then add to the lentils. Add salt to taste.

DRY SPROUTED GREEN LENTIL TORAN
(Moong Dal Toran)

INGREDIENTS (Serves 4)
2 Tbsp oil
¼ tsp asafoetida
1 tsp chili powder
½ tsp turmeric
1 tsp ground coriander
½ tsp ground cumin
1lb sprouted green lentils
salt
leaves from 1 sprig of coriander
1 tsp lemon juice

1 Heat the oil in a pan, add the asafoetida, chili powder, turmeric, ground coriander and cumin, and fry for a few minutes until the fragrance emerges.

2 Add the sprouted lentils together with 2 Tbsp water, ½ tsp salt and half the coriander leaves. Cook, covered, over low heat, stirring occasionally, for about 10 minutes or until the sprouted lentils are cooked and almost all the water has evaporated.

3 Sprinkle on the lemon juice and the remaining coriander leaves. Add extra salt to taste.

GREEN LENTIL AND BANANA CURRY
(Kela Moong Curry)

INGREDIENTS (Serves 2)
¾ cup whole green lentils (moong dal)
1 or 2 hard green bananas, peeled and sliced
½ tsp turmeric
1 green chili pepper, chopped
salt
1⅓ cups grated fresh or dried unsweetened
  coconut
½ tsp ground cumin
2 Tbsp oil
1 tsp mustard seeds
4-6 curry leaves

1 Pick over the lentils, wash thoroughly and cook in about 3¾ cups water for about 30 minutes until nearly done.

2 Add the banana, turmeric, chili and ½ tsp salt, and continue to cook over low heat.

3 In a blender or food processor, blend the coconut with the cumin and 1-2 Tbsp water to make a thick paste. Add to the lentils. Stir and cook for 3 minutes to heat through. Add a little water, if necessary, to make a thick sauce.

4 Heat the oil in a skillet and, when hot, add the mustard seeds and the curry leaves. Let them sizzle for a few seconds until all the seeds have popped, then add to the curry. Add extra salt to taste.

ABOVE Spiced Chick-peas
(Masala Chana)
See page 33

OPPOSITE Chick-peas with Mango
and Coconut
(Aam aur Nariel Ke Chana)
See page 36

VEGETABLES
Sabzi

India grows a huge variety of vegetables, and combinations of vegetables and spices are endless. Sometimes the spices are used to make a thick sauce, and at other times the vegetables are cooked "dry" (toran) so that the spices stick to them, making a tasty, crunchy crust. Hot, spicy vegetables are usually served with rice and mild, fragrant ones with bread.

Potatoes and peas are the vegetables most commonly used, with yam (sweet potato) and pumpkin coming next. White pumpkin is not found as commonly as the red variety; instead you can use the *dhoody* and *doddy* (*poo gwa* in Chinese markets) a vegetable that has the shape of a small squash, but the coloring and smoothness of a turnip. The red pumpkin is known as *calabaza* in Latin American grocery stores.

Vegetables like okra and bitter melon — a distorted cone-shaped pod with a skin as gnarled as a walnut — are now becoming more widely available. Drumsticks are still to be had only in Indian grocery stores — these are slim, ridged vegetables up to 1 foot long, which need to be peeled and cut into suitable lengths before cooking. They are always available in cans in Indian grocery stores.

Just as vegetables can be used in the making of sweet desserts, fruit can be used in curry; banana and plantain are popular curry ingredients.

BUTTERMILK CURRY (Morkari)

INGREDIENTS (Serves 4)
2 cups peeled and cubed red pumpkin or
    butternut squash
2 cups peeled and cubed potatoes
1 hard green banana, peeled and thickly sliced
½ tsp turmeric
½ tsp chili powder
2 tsp salt
grated flesh of ½ coconut
½ tsp ground cumin
2½ cups buttermilk
2 Tbsp oil
1 tsp mustard seeds
½ tsp fenugreek seeds
1 or 2 red chili peppers, cut into 3 or 4 pieces
6-8 curry leaves

1. Simmer the pumpkin, potato and banana in a pot of water with the turmeric, chili powder and 1 tsp salt for 10-15 minutes, until cooked. Drain and keep hot.

2. In a bowl, blend the coconut with the cumin, then stir in the buttermilk.

3. Stir the buttermilk mixture into the vegetables over a low heat. Cook for 3-4 minutes, until heated through, stirring all the time so that the buttermilk does not separate. Set aside, covered.

4. Heat the oil in a skillet and add the mustard seeds, fenugreek seeds and red chili. Let them sizzle for a few seconds until all the mustard seeds have popped. Add to the curry.

5. Add salt to taste and sprinkle on the curry leaves.

EXTRA THICK BUTTERMILK CURRY (Kalan)

INGREDIENTS (Serves 4-6)
2 cups peeled and cubed yam
1 green plantain, peeled and cubed
2 cups peeled and cubed white or red
    pumpkin or butternut squash
½ tsp turmeric
½ tsp chili powder
grated flesh of 1 small coconut
½ tsp ground cumin
½ tsp ground white pepper
2½ cups buttermilk
2 green chili peppers, cut in half
2 Tbsp oil
1 tsp mustard seeds
2 red chili peppers, cut into 3 or 4 pieces
½ tsp fenugreek seeds
8 curry leaves
2 Tbsp sugar
2 tsp salt

1. Cook the yam, plantain and pumpkin with the turmeric and chili powder in water to cover over low heat for about 10 minutes, until tender but not soft.

2 Blend the coconut, cumin and pepper and mix well with the buttermilk, then add to the pan with the vegetables and green chilis. Heat through over low heat for 3-4 minutes, stirring briskly to prevent the buttermilk from separating.

3 Heat the oil in a pan, add the mustard seeds, red chili, fenugreek seeds and half the curry leaves and let them sizzle for a few seconds, until all the seeds have popped.
Stir into the curry with the remaining curry leaves, the sugar and salt to taste.

(Photograph, see page 42)

RIPE MANGO CURRY I
(Aam Curry)

INGREDIENTS (Serves 4-6)
2 cups peeled and cubed yam or potato
2 hard green plantains, peeled and cubed
½ tsp turmeric
½ tsp chili powder
2 green chili peppers, cut into 4 pieces
4 small sweet ripe mangoes, peeled and cubed
grated flesh of ½ coconut
½ tsp cumin seeds
1 cup yogurt
2 Tbsp oil
½ tsp mustard seeds
½ tsp fenugreek seeds
1 red chili pepper, cut into 4 pieces
salt

1 Cook the yam or potato and plantain in water to cover with the turmeric, chili powder and green chili for about 6-7 minutes, until half cooked.

2 Add the mango and continue to cook for a further 6-7 minutes, until the vegetables are tender.

3 Meanwhile, blend the coconut and cumin seeds and stir into the yogurt.

4 Drain the vegetables, stir in the yogurt and cook over low heat, stirring to keep the yogurt from separating, for 3-4 minutes, until heated through. Cover and set aside.

5 Heat the oil in a skillet and add the mustard seeds, fenugreek seeds and red chili pepper. Let them sizzle for a few seconds until all the mustard seeds have popped, then add to the curry. Add salt to taste.

(Photograph, see page 43)

ABOVE Extra Thick Buttermilk
Curry
(Kalan)
See page 40

OPPOSITE Ripe Mango Curry I
(Aam Curry)
See page 41

RIPE MANGO CURRY II
(Aam Curry)

INGREDIENTS (Serves 4)
4 small sweet ripe mangoes, cubed, with the
skin left on
2 tsp chili powder
½ tsp turmeric
salt
grated flesh of ½ coconut
½ tsp ground cumin
6 curry leaves
2 Tbsp oil
2 tsp mustard seeds
2 tsp fenugreek seeds
2 red chili peppers, cut into 4 pieces
2-3 tsp sugar

1 Cook the mango in about 2½ cups water with the chili powder, turmeric and 1 tsp salt for about 5 minutes, making sure that the mango does not lose its shape.

2 Blend the coconut with the cumin and add to the mango with half the curry leaves.

3 Heat the oil in a skillet and, when hot, add the mustard seeds. Let them sizzle for a few seconds until they have all popped, then add the fenugreek seeds, red chili pepper and remaining curry leaves. Stir and fry for a few seconds, then add to the mango. Stir well and add sugar and salt to taste.

MIXED VEGETABLE CURRY
(Aviyal)

INGREDIENTS (Serves 4-6)
1 hard green banana, unpeeled
½ cup green beans, trimmed
8oz yam or potato, peeled
4oz white pumpkin (see page 40) or green
papaya, peeled
½ tsp chili powder
salt
1 Tbsp tamarind juice (see page 19)
2 green chili peppers
3 Tbsp grated fresh coconut
6-8 curry leaves
1 cup yogurt
2 Tbsp coconut oil
a little sugar, optional

1 Cook the banana and vegetables in water to cover with the chili powder and ½ tsp salt for about 15 minutes, until tender but not soft, stirring occasionally with a wooden spoon. Add the tamarind juice and set aside, covered.

2 Cut the chilis into 4 and crush them with the grated coconut and curry leaves. Stir in the yogurt and add to the vegetables, mixing well.

3 Mix the coconut oil with a little water to release its fragrance. Pour over the vegetables and add salt to taste. Mix again and add a little sugar, if desired.
(Photograph, see page 46)

VEGETABLE CURRY WITH COCONUT MILK
(*Sabzi Nariel*)

INGREDIENTS (Serves 4)
flesh of 1 coconut, grated
1lb ripe white pumpkin, peeled and cubed
1 Tbsp coconut oil, mixed with 1 Tbsp water
4-6 curry leaves
salt

1 Blend the coconut in a blender with 1 Tbsp boiling water. Transfer to a piece of cheesecloth and squeeze out the milk into a bowl. Return the coconut to the blender, add another Tbsp boiling water and repeat the process, straining the milk into a separate bowl.

2 Cook the pumpkin in water to cover over low heat for about 10 minutes, until tender, then add the second bowl of coconut milk and bring to a boil. Remove the pan from the heat.

3 Stir in the first bowl of coconut milk. Add the coconut oil, curry leaves and salt to taste.

VEGETABLE CURRY WITH ROASTED COCONUT
(*Eliseri*)

INGREDIENTS (Serves 2-3)
½ cup toor dal
1lb red pumpkin or butter nut squash
 (see page 40), cubed
1 tsp chili powder
½ tsp turmeric
salt
⅔-1 cup grated fresh or dried unsweetened
 coconut
1 tsp ground cumin
6-8 curry leaves
4 Tbsp oil
1 tsp mustard seeds
2 red chili peppers, cut into pieces

1 Pick over the dal, wash thoroughly and cook in about 5 cups water for about 15 minutes, until you can mash it with the back of a wooden spoon.

2 Meanwhile, cook the pumpkin in water for about 12 minutes, until tender.

3 Drain the dal and the pumpkin, reserving a little of the cooking liquor, and mix the two together with the chili powder, turmeric and ½ tsp salt. Cook over low heat, stirring, for 3-4 minutes, adding a little of the cooking liquor if the mixture threatens to stick. Cover and set aside.

4 Blend half the coconut with the cumin and half the curry leaves. Stir into the curry.

5 Heat the oil in a skillet and, when hot, add the mustard seeds and red chili. Let them sizzle for a few seconds until all the mustard seeds have popped. Add the remaining grated coconut and curry leaves and fry, stirring briskly, for a few seconds until the fragrance of roasted coconut emerges.

6 Fold the fried spice mixture into the curry and add salt to taste.

VEGETABLE CURRY, TAMIL STYLE
(*Sambar*)

INGREDIENTS (Serves 4-6)
1½ cups toor dal
4 drumsticks (see page 40)
1 eggplant
2 medium potatoes
1 medium onion, quartered and sliced
½ tsp turmeric
salt
4 Tbsp tamarind juice (see page 19)
3-4 Tbsp sambar powder (see page 22)
1 tomato, cut into 8 pieces
1 Tbsp oil
1 tsp mustard seeds
4-6 curry leaves
2 tsp sugar
leaves from 1 sprig of coriander

1 Pick over the dal, wash thoroughly and cook in about 5 cups water for about 15 minutes, until you can mash it with the back of a wooden spoon.

2 Meanwhile, peel the drumsticks and chop into 2 inch lengths. Peel the eggplant and potatoes and cut into cubes, dropping them into a pan of water as you go to prevent discoloration.

3 Add the eggplant, potato and onion to the cooked dal, with a little extra water if necessary, and cook for about 8 minutes, until the vegetables are half-cooked.

4 Add the drumsticks, turmeric and ½ tsp salt and continue cooking for about 10 minutes, until the vegetables are tender.

5 Stir in the tamarind juice, sambar powder and tomato; cover and keep hot.

6 Heat the oil in a pan and add the mustard seeds and curry leaves. Let them sizzle for a few seconds, until all the mustard seeds have popped, then add to the curry.

7 Stir in sugar and salt to taste and garnish with coriander leaves.

RIGHT Mixed Vegetable Curry
(Aviyal)
See page 44

VEGETABLE CURRY, KERALA STYLE
(Sambar)

INGREDIENTS (Serves 4-6)
1½ cups toor dal
½ tsp turmeric
4-6oz okra, trimmed and cut into
*   1 inch lengths*
4 Tbsp oil
1 medium onion, quartered and sliced
2 cups cubed potatoes
2 tomatoes, peeled and chopped
2 Tbsp tamarind juice (see page 19)
1⅓ cups grated fresh coconut
4-6 curry leaves
2 Tbsp sambar powder
1 tsp mustard seeds
1 red chili pepper, cut into 4 pieces
salt
coriander leaves, to garnish

1 Pick over the dal, wash thoroughly and cook in about 5 cups water with the turmeric for about 15 minutes, until you can mash it with the back of a wooden spoon.

2 Meanwhile, fry the okra in 1 Tbsp oil, turning gently, until all the oil is absorbed. This seals the okra and helps it keep its shape. Set aside.

3 When the dal is ready, stir in the onion and potato and continue to cook gently over low heat for about 8 minutes, until the vegetables are half-cooked.

4 Add the tomato and okra and cook for a further 10 minutes, until the vegetables are tender, adding a little extra water if the pot threatens to boil dry.

5 Stir in the tamarind juice, cover and keep hot.

6 Fry the coconut and half the curry leaves in 1 Tbsp oil, then blend with the sambar powder and add to the vegetables.

7 Heat the remaining oil, add the mustard seeds and the red chili and let them sizzle for a few seconds until all the mustard seeds have popped. Add to the curry.

8 Stir in salt to taste and garnish with coriander leaves.

(Photograph, see page 51)

POTATO CURRY
(*Aloo Dum*)

INGREDIENTS (Serves 2)
2 cups peeled and cubed potatoes
1 Tbsp finely grated fresh ginger
1 green chili pepper, chopped
1 onion, thinly sliced
½ tsp turmeric
½ tsp chili powder
⅔ cup grated fresh coconut
1 Tbsp oil
1 tsp mustard seeds
4 curry leaves
salt

1 Cook the potato in water to cover with the ginger, green chili pepper, onion, turmeric and chili powder for about 15 minutes, until tender but not soft.

2 Meanwhile, purée the coconut in a blender and add to the potato.

3 Heat the oil in a pan and add the mustard seeds and curry leaves. Let them sizzle for a few seconds until all the seeds have popped, then add to the potato.

4 Let stand, tightly covered, for 5-10 minutes, then add salt to taste.

DRY SPICED POTATO
(*Aloo Masala*)

INGREDIENTS (Serves 4)
1lb new potatoes
½ cup butter or ghee
1 onion, chopped
1 Tbsp finely grated fresh ginger
2 cloves garlic, finely chopped
leaves from 1 sprig of coriander
¾ cup peeled and chopped tomatoes
½ tsp garam masala
½ tsp chili powder
½ tsp mango powder (amchur)
salt
½ tsp ground cumin

1 Scrub the potatoes and cut into quarters. Put them in a pan of cold water to prevent discoloration.

2 Heat three-quarters of the butter or ghee in a pan and add the onion, ginger, garlic and half the coriander leaves. Fry until the onion turns golden.

3 Add the tomato, garam masala, chili powder and mango powder, stirring well to mix and crushing the tomato with the back of a wooden spoon to make a paste.

4 Drain the potato and add to the pan with 1-2 Tbsp water. Cover and cook over low heat for about 20 minutes, until the potato is tender but not soft, and all the water has been absorbed. Add salt to taste.

5 Heat the remaining butter or ghee in a separate pan and fry the cumin for 3-4 minutes until the fragrance emerges. Add to the cooked potato and garnish with the remaining coriander leaves.

(Photograph, see page 50)

ABOVE Vegetable Curry, Kerala
Style
(Sambar)
See page 48

OPPOSITE Dry Spiced Potato
(Aloo Masala)
See page 49

POTATO MASALA CURRY
(Aloo Masala)

INGREDIENTS (Serves 4)
3 or 4 medium potatoes, cubed
1 large onion, finely chopped
½ tsp turmeric
salt
2 green chili peppers, chopped
2 tsp garam masala
2 Tbsp grated fresh or dried unsweetened
*   coconut*
1 Tbsp finely grated fresh ginger
2 Tbsp oil
1 tsp mustard seeds
4-6 curry leaves
leaves from 1 sprig of coriander

1 Cook the potato in just enough water to cover with three-quarters of the onion, the turmeric, ½ tsp salt and the green chili, for about 8 minutes, until half cooked.

2 Meanwhile, purée the garam masala, coconut and ginger in a blender or food processor. Add to the potato and continue to cook for 8 minutes, until tender but not soft.

3 Heat the oil in a skillet and add the mustard seeds. Let them sizzle for a few seconds until they have all popped, then add the remaining chopped onion and fry until golden. Stir into the curry.

4 Add salt to taste and sprinkle on the curry and coriander leaves.

(Photograph, see page 54)

POTATO CURRY WITH COCONUT MILK
(Aloo Nariel)

INGREDIENTS (Serves 4)
flesh of 1 coconut, grated
1lb potatoes, cubed
2 cups chopped onion
1 Tbsp finely grated fresh ginger
2 green chili peppers, sliced
salt
4-6 curry leaves
2 Tbsp coconut oil

1 Purée the coconut in a blender or food processor with 1 Tbsp boiling water. Transfer to a piece of cheesecloth and squeeze out the milk into a bowl. Return the coconut to the blender or food processor, add another Tbsp boiling water and repeat the process, straining the milk into a separate bowl.

2 Put the potato and onion in a pan with the second batch of coconut milk, adding water to cover if necessary. Add the ginger, green chili and 1 tsp salt and cook for about 15 minutes.

3 Add the curry leaves and the coconut oil mixed with 1 Tbsp water to release its fragrance. Remove from the heat and stir in the remaining coconut milk.

PUMPKIN AND POTATO CURRY
(Aloo Pethi)

INGREDIENTS (Serves 2)
1 Tbsp sambar powder
1 cup peeled and cubed potato
2 cups peeled and cubed unripe red pumpkin
  (see page 40) or butternut squash
2 Tbsp oil
1/2 tsp mustard seeds
1 small onion, chopped
4-6 curry leaves
1/4 tsp asafoetida
1/2 tsp turmeric
1 red chili pepper
1/2 cup peeled and chopped tomatoes
salt

1 Sprinkle the sambar powder over the potato and pumpkin. Stir well to coat and set aside.

2 Heat the oil in a pan and add the mustard seeds. Let them sizzle for a few seconds until they have all popped, then add the onion, curry leaves, asafoetida, turmeric and red chili. Stir well and fry until the onion is golden.

3 Add the marinated vegetables, the tomato and enough water to just cover. Simmer for about 15 minutes over a low heat, until the vegetables are tender but not soft and the sauce is thick. Add salt to taste.

RIPE PLANTAIN CURRY WITH YOGURT
(Kela Dahi)

INGREDIENTS (Serves 4)
2 or 3 ripe plantains, peeled and thickly sliced
1/2 tsp chili powder
1/2 tsp turmeric
4-6 Tbsp grated fresh or dried unsweetened
  coconut
1/2 tsp cumin seeds or ground cumin
1 cup yogurt
2 Tbsp oil
1 tsp mustard seeds
1 red chili pepper, cut into 3 or 4 pieces
6-8 curry leaves
3 Tbsp brown sugar
salt

1 Cook the plantain in about 2 1/2 cups water with the chili powder and turmeric for 5 minutes, until it is tender but not soft and most of the water has evaporated.

2 Grind or pound the coconut with the cumin (or blend in a blender or food processor), then mix with the yogurt in a bowl.

3 Stir the yogurt into the plantain over low heat. Cook for 3-4 minutes to heat through, stirring all the time to prevent the yogurt from separating. Cover and set aside.

4 Heat the oil in a pan and, when hot, add the mustard seeds. Let them sizzle for a few seconds until they have all popped, then add the red chili and half the curry leaves. Continue to fry for a few seconds, then add to the curry.

5 Stir in sugar and salt to taste and sprinkle with the remaining curry leaves.

MUSTARD CURRY
(Pachadi)

INGREDIENTS (Serves 4)
4-6 Tbsp grated fresh or dried unsweetened
  coconut
2-3 green chili peppers, sliced
2 tsp mustard seeds
1 cup yoghurt
1lb unripe red pumpkin (see page 40),
  butternut squash or ripe green papaya,
  cubed
2 Tbsp oil
1 red chili pepper, chopped
4-6 curry leaves
2 tsp sugar
salt

1 Grind or pound the coconut, green chili and half the mustard seeds into a fine paste, then mix with the yogurt.

2 Cook the pumpkin or papaya in just enough water to cover for about 15 minutes, until it is tender, and most of the water has evaporated.

3 Stir in the yogurt over low heat. Cook for 3-4 minutes to heat through, stirring all the time to prevent the yogurt from separating.

4 Heat the oil in a pan and fry the remaining mustard seeds. Let them sizzle for a few seconds until they have all popped, then add the red chili and curry leaves. Continue to fry, stirring, for a few seconds, then add to the curry. Add sugar and salt to taste.

RIGHT Potato Masala Curry
(Aloo Masala)
See page 52

GREEN BEANS AND POTATO TORAN
(Aloo Hari Moong Toran)

INGREDIENTS (Serves 2)
¼-⅓ cup butter or ghee
1 small onion, finely chopped
1 cup peeled and finely chopped tomatoes
½ tsp garam masala
½ tsp turmeric
½ tsp chili powder
8oz green beans, trimmed and cut into
    1-inch lengths
2 cups peeled and diced potatoes
1 green chili pepper, cut into pieces
1 Tbsp finely grated fresh ginger
1 clove garlic, finely chopped
leaves from 1 sprig of coriander
salt

1 Heat the butter or ghee in a large saucepan and fry the onion until golden.

2 Add the tomato, stir well and mash with the back of a wooden spoon until it forms a paste.

3 Add the garam masala, turmeric and chili powder and continue to fry, stirring, for about 5 minutes.

4 Add the beans, potatoes, green chili, ginger, garlic and coriander leaves with 1 Tbsp water and cook gently over low heat, tightly covered, stirring occasionally, for 10-15 minutes, until the vegetables are done. Add salt to taste.

(Photograph, see page 59)

GREEN BEANS TORAN I
(Hari Moong Toran)

INGREDIENTS (Serves 2)
1 Tbsp oil
1 tsp mustard seeds
1 red chili pepper, cut into 4 or 6 pieces
4-6 curry leaves
1 small onion, finely chopped
8oz green beans, trimmed and cut into
    1-inch lengths
salt
⅔-1 cup grated fresh coconut

1 Heat the oil in a heavy-bottomed saucepan and, when hot, add the mustard seeds. Let them sizzle for a few seconds until they have all popped.

2 Add the red chili, curry leaves and onion and fry gently, stirring, until the onion is golden.

3 Turn the heat to low and add the beans, 1 Tbsp water, ½ tsp salt and the coconut. Cook, tightly covered, for about 10 minutes, until the beans are tender but not soft, stirring occasionally.

4 Let the pot stand for about 5 minutes and add extra salt if necessary before serving.

GREEN BEANS TORAN II
(Hari Moong Toran)

INGREDIENTS (Serves 2)
1 or 2 green chili peppers, chopped
1 cup grated fresh coconut
4-6 curry leaves
1 clove garlic, chopped
8oz green beans, trimmed and cut into
   1-inch lengths
1/2 tsp turmeric
2 Tbsp oil
2 tsp polished split black lentils (urid dal)
1 tsp mustard seeds
salt

1 Crush the green chili with the coconut, curry leaves and garlic and mix with the green beans and turmeric in a heavy-bottomed saucepan. Add 1-2 Tbsp water and cook over very low heat, covered tightly, for 10-15 minutes, until tender. Stir occasionally to prevent sticking.

2 Heat the oil in a pan, add the dal and fry until golden.

3 Add the mustard seeds and let them sizzle for a few seconds until they have all popped. Add to the beans and cook for a further 3-4 minutes.

4 Let the pot stand off the heat, covered, for 3-4 minutes, then add salt to taste.

DRY SPICED CABBAGE
(Gobi Bhaji)

INGREDIENTS (Serves 4)
1lb cabbage
8oz potatoes
2 Tbsp oil
1/2 tsp ground cumin
1/2 tsp ground coriander
1/2 tsp turmeric
1/4 tsp asafoetida
1/2 tsp chili powder
salt

1 Cut the cabbage into strips; peel and finely chop the potatoes.

2 Heat the oil and fry the cumin, coriander, turmeric, asafoetida and chili powder for 3-4 minutes, until the fragrance of the spices emerges.

3 Add the cabbage and potato, sprinkle on 1-2 Tbsp water and 1/2 tsp salt, cover the pan tightly and cook on a low heat for 5-6 minutes, until the potato is cooked.

4 Take the pot off the heat and let it stand, covered, for 3-4 minutes. Add extra salt to taste.

(Photograph, see page 58)

ABOVE Green Beans and Potato
Toran
(Aloo Hari Moong Toran)
See page 56

OPPOSITE Dry Spiced Cabbage
(Gobi Bhaji)
See page 57

CABBAGE TORAN
(Gobi Toran)

INGREDIENTS (Serves 2)
2 Tbsp oil
1-2 tsp polished split black lentils (urid dal)
½ tsp mustard seeds
4-6 curry leaves
1 small onion, finely chopped
1 green chili pepper, sliced
1 Tbsp finely grated fresh ginger
1lb cabbage, very finely chopped or grated
½ tsp turmeric
⅔-1 cup grated fresh coconut
salt

1 Heat the oil in a pan big enough to hold the cabbage. Add the dal and fry until golden.

2 Add the mustard seeds and let them sizzle for a few seconds until they have all popped.

3 Add the curry leaves, onion, green chili and ginger and continue to fry, stirring, for 3-4 minutes.

4 Stir the cabbage into the pan with the turmeric, cover tightly and cook for about 4 minutes over low heat until tender but not soft.

5 Stir in the grated coconut and add salt to taste.

MASHED EGGPLANT
(Baigan Bharta)

INGREDIENTS (Serves 2)
1 eggplant
¼-⅓ cup butter or ghee
1 onion, finely chopped
leaves from 1 sprig of coriander
1 clove garlic, chopped
1 Tbsp finely grated, fresh ginger
½ tsp garam masala
1 green chili pepper, sliced
½ tsp turmeric
½ tsp cumin
½ tsp chili powder
1 cup peeled and chopped, tomatoes
salt
1 Tbsp lemon juice

1 Put the eggplant in a roasting pan and bake in a preheated 400°F oven for 40 minutes or until cooked through. Allow the eggplant to cool, then peel off the skin and immerse the vegetable in cold water.

2 Heat the butter or ghee in a pan and add the onion, half the coriander leaves, the garlic, ginger, garam masala, green chili, turmeric, cumin and chili powder. Stir and fry until the onion is golden.

3 Add the tomatoes, mashing well with the back of a wooden spoon to make a paste.

4 Meanwhile, drain the eggplant and mash with a fork.

5 When the butter runs out of the spice paste, add the eggplant and ½ tsp salt, stir thoroughly and cook for 3-4 minutes to heat through.

6 Sprinkle on the remaining coriander leaves and the lemon juice. Add more salt to taste if desired.

(Photograph, see page 62)

EGGPLANT AND POTATO TORAN
(*Baigan Aloo Toran*)

INGREDIENTS (Serves 4)
3 cups small eggplants
8oz potatoes
1 Tbsp finely grated fresh ginger
2 cloves garlic, chopped
leaves from 1 sprig of coriander
1 tsp ground coriander
½ tsp chili powder
½ tsp garam masala
½ tsp turmeric
juice from 1-2 Tbsp seedless tamarind
*   (see page 19)*
1 small onion, finely chopped
2 Tbsp oil
salt

1 Cut the eggplants into large chunks; peel and cube the potatoes and leave the vegetables in a bowl of cold water to prevent discoloration while you prepare the spices.

2 In a blender or food processor, blend together the ginger, garlic, coriander leaves, powdered spices, tamarind juice and onion.

3 Heat the oil in a frying pan and add the blended spices. Stir and fry for 3-4 minutes, until the oil runs clear of the spices.

4 Drain the vegetables, add them to the pan and cook, tightly covered, over low heat for 15-20 minutes, until tender. Add 1-2 Tbsp water during the cooking if necessary and stir occasionally to prevent the vegetables from sticking.

5 Add salt to taste.

STUFFED OKRA
(*Sabu Bhindi*)

INGREDIENTS (Serves 2)
8oz okra
½ tsp paprika
½ tsp chili powder
1 Tbsp mango powder (amchur)
½ tsp ground ginger
salt
5 Tbsp oil

1 Wash the okra and dry on paper towels. Cut off the stems and cut the okra in half lengthwise.

2 Mix together the spices and salt.

3 Stuff the okra with the spice mix and let them stand in a cool place for at least 30 minutes.

4 Heat the oil and fry the okra for about 4 minutes, turning carefully to cook on all sides.

(Photograph, see page 63)

ABOVE Mashed Eggplant
(Baigan Bharta)
See page 60

ABOVE Stuffed Okra
(Sabu Bhindi)
See page 61

OKRA TORAN
(Bhindi Toran)

INGREDIENTS (Serves 2)
10oz okra
3 Tbsp oil
½ tsp mustard seeds
1 tsp polished split black lentils (urid dal)
1 small onion, chopped
1 Tbsp finely grated, fresh ginger
2 green chili peppers, chopped
⅓–⅔ cup grated fresh or dried unsweetened
  coconut
4-6 curry leaves
salt

1 Wash the okra and dry on paper towels. Cut into ¾-inch lengths.

2 Fry the okra in 2 Tbsp oil, turning frequently, until all the oil has been absorbed. This seals the okra and helps them keep their shape during cooking. Remove the okra from the pan with a slotted spoon and set aside.

3 Add the remaining oil to the pan and, when hot, add the mustard seeds and dal. Let them sizzle for a few seconds until all the mustard seeds have popped and the dal is golden, then add the onion and fry until golden.

4 Add the ginger and green chili and continue to fry for 3-4 minutes, then add the okra and fry for a further 3-4 minutes. Stir in the coconut and curry leaves. Add salt to taste.

OKRA CURRY
(Bhindi Curry)

INGREDIENTS (Serves 2)
8oz okra
4 Tbsp oil
grated flesh of ½ coconut
½ tsp chili powder
½ tsp turmeric
½ tsp ground cumin
1 cup yogurt
½ tsp mustard seeds
1 red chili pepper, cut into pieces
leaves from 1 sprig of coriander, chopped
4-6 curry leaves
salt

1 Wash the okra and dry them on paper towels. Cut into 1-inch lengths.

2 Heat 1 Tbsp oil and fry the okra for about 2 minutes, turning gently, until all the oil has been absorbed. Remove with a slotted spoon and set aside.

3 Blend the coconut with the chili powder, turmeric and cumin in a blender or food processor, adding 1 Tbsp water to make a smooth paste. Mix this into the yogurt.

4 Heat the remaining oil and, when hot, add the mustard seeds and red chili. Let them sizzle for a few seconds, until all the seeds have popped, then add the okra.

5 Turn the heat down and add the yogurt mix. Cook gently for 2-3 minutes, stirring to prevent the yogurt from separating, until heated through. Add the coriander and curry leaves, and salt to taste.

FRIED SPICED OKRA
(Bhindi Masala)

INGREDIENTS (Serves 2)
8oz okra
¼ cup butter or ghee
1 small onion, finely chopped
1 clove garlic, finely chopped
1 green chili pepper, chopped
1 Tbsp finely grated fresh ginger
leaves from 1 sprig of coriander
½ cup peeled and coarsely chopped tomatoes
½ tsp ground coriander
½ tsp turmeric
½ tsp chili powder
1 tsp garam masala
salt

1 Wash the okra and dry them on paper towels. Cut into l-inch lengths. Heat half the butter or ghee in a pan, add the okra and fry gently. Keep turning them until most of the fat has been absorbed and they are cooked on all sides (about 2 minutes). Remove with a slotted spoon and set aside.

2 Add the remaining butter or ghee to the pan and, when hot, add the onion, garlic, green chili, ginger and coriander leaves. Stir and fry until the onion is golden.

3 Add the tomato, ground coriander, turmeric, chili powder and garam masala and continue to cook, mashing the tomato with the back of a wooden spoon to make a paste.

4 When the butter runs clear of the spices, add the okra and cook over low heat, stirring occasionally, for about 10 minutes. Add salt to taste.

STUFFED BITTER MELON
(Sabu Karela)

INGREDIENTS (Serves 4)
1lb bitter melons
1 tsp salt
1 tsp chili powder
2 Tbsp mango powder (amchur)
5 Tbsp oil

| 1 | Scrape the melons and slit them lengthwise from the tip, leaving the 2 halves joined at the stem. Sprinkle salt both inside and out and leave the melons in a cool place for 15 minutes. |

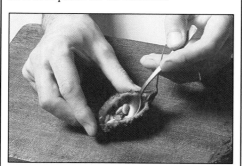

| 2 | Scrape away the seeds and squeeze the melons to remove the moisture drawn from them by the salt. |

| 3 | Mix together the chili powder, mango powder and remaining salt. |

| 4 | Sprinkle the insides of the melons with oil and stuff the spice mixture well down inside them. Tie the melons closed with thread. |

| 5 | Heat the remaining oil over a low heat and fry the melons, turning gently for 5-10 minutes, until cooked. Remove thread. |

| 6 | Serve hot or cold. |

(Photograph, see page 67)

BITTER MELON WITH ONION STUFFING
(Piyaz Karela)

INGREDIENTS (Serves 2)
8oz bitter melons
salt
1 onion, finely chopped
1 tsp chili powder
1 Tbsp finely grated fresh ginger
2 Tbsp lemon juice
5 Tbsp oil

| 1 | Scrape the melons and slit them lengthwise from the tip, leaving the 2 halves joined at the stem. Sprinkle salt both inside and out and leave the melons in a cool place for 15 minutes. |

| 2 | Scrape away the seeds and squeeze the melons to remove the moisture drawn from them by the salt. |

| 3 | In a blender or food processor, blend together the onion, chili powder, ½ tsp salt and the ginger, then mix in the lemon juice. |

| 4 | Stuff the melons with the onion mixture and tie them closed with thread. Let stand for 5-10 minutes. |

| 5 | Heat the oil in a pan, add the melons and fry over low heat, turning gently, for 5-10 minutes, until done. |

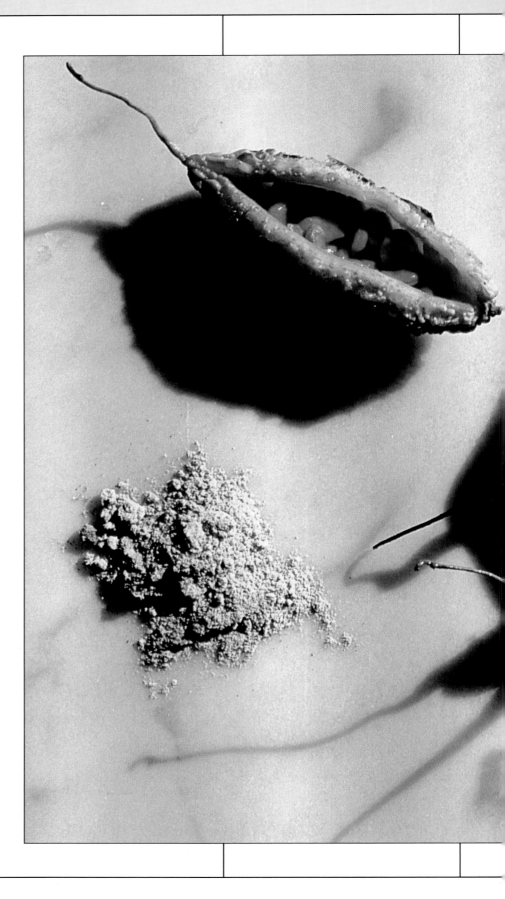

RIGHT Stuffed Bitter Melons
(Sabu Karela)
See page 65

FRIED BITTER MELON
(Karela Masala)

8oz bitter melons
salt
5 Tbsp oil
1 green chili, sliced
1 Tbsp finely grated fresh ginger
6-8 curry leaves
2 Tbsp lemon juice

1 Peel the melons and cut into ¾inch slices. Sprinkle with 1 tsp salt and let stand in a cool place for 10 minutes. Rinse carefully and dry on paper towels.

2 Heat the oil in a pan and add the melons, green chili, ginger and curry leaves. Fry for 10-15 minutes, stirring, until the melon is cooked.

3 Sprinkle with the lemon juice and add salt to taste.

(Photograph, see page 71)

CAULIFLOWER WITH COCONUT MILK
(Nariel Phul Gobi)

INGREDIENTS (Serves 4)
flesh of 1 coconut, grated
1lb cauliflower, cut into florets, tough stems discarded
1 cup peeled and cubed potatoes
1 Tbsp finely grated fresh ginger
½ tsp turmeric
½ tsp sambar powder (see page 22)
1 small onion, finely chopped
1 green chili pepper, sliced
4-6 curry leaves
2-3 Tbsp oil
1 tsp mustard seeds
salt
leaves from 1 sprig of coriander

1 Purée the coconut in a blender or food processor with 1 Tbsp boiling water. Transfer to a square of cheesecloth and squeeze the milk into a bowl. Return the coconut to the blender or food processor and repeat the process.

2 Simmer the cauliflower and potato in the coconut milk with the ginger, turmeric, sambar powder, three-quarters of the onion and the chili for about 12 minutes, until the vegetables are tender but not soft. Add the curry leaves.

3 Meanwhile, heat the oil in a pan and, when hot, add the mustard seeds. Let them sizzle for a few seconds until they have all popped.

4 Add the remaining onion and fry until golden, then add to the curry.

5 Add salt to taste and garnish with coriander leaves.

CAULIFLOWER WITH COCONUT AND SPICES
(Nariel Phul Gobi Masala)

INGREDIENTS (Serves 4)
1 medium potato
1lb cauliflower
1⅓ cups grated fresh coconut
1 green chili pepper
1 Tbsp finely grated fresh ginger
1 clove garlic, finely chopped
leaves from 1 sprig of coriander
½ tsp turmeric
1 small onion, finely chopped
4 cashew nuts
2 Tbsp oil
1 tsp mustard seeds
4-6 curry leaves
1 red chili pepper, cut into 4 pieces
½ cup chopped tomatoes
2 tsp lemon juice
salt

1 Peel the potato and cut into chunks. Divide the cauliflower into florets, discarding the tough stems. Put the vegetables in a bowl of cold water to prevent discoloration.

2 In a blender or food processor, coarsely purée the coconut, green chili, ginger, garlic, coriander leaves, turmeric, onion and cashew nuts.

3 Drain the vegetables, turn them in the spice mixture to coat and let stand for about 10 minutes to absorb the flavors.

4 Heat the oil in a pan and, when hot, add the mustard seeds, half the curry leaves and the red chili. Leave them to sizzle for a few seconds until all the seeds have popped.

5 Add the spiced vegetables and tomatoes to the pan, cover and cook over low heat, stirring occasionally, for about 10 minutes, until the potato is tender but not soft.

6 Sprinkle with the lemon juice, stir in the remaining curry leaves and add salt to taste.

CAULIFLOWER WITH POTATO AND TOMATOES
(Aloo Gobi Tamatar Masala)

INGREDIENTS (Serves 4)
1 medium potato
1lb cauliflower
¼ cup butter or ghee
1 small onion, finely chopped
1 Tbsp finely grated fresh ginger
1 clove garlic, finely chopped
2 green chili peppers, cut into 4-6 pieces
leaves from 1 sprig of coriander
½ cup peeled and coarsely chopped tomatoes
½ tsp chili powder
½ tsp turmeric
½ tsp ground coriander
½ tsp fennel seeds
½ tsp garam masala
1 tsp ground cumin
salt

1 Peel the potato and cut into chunks. Divide the cauliflower into florets, discarding the tough stems. Put the vegetables in a bowl of cold water to prevent discoloration.

2 Heat three-quarters of the butter or ghee in a heavy-bottomed pan and add the onion, ginger, garlic, green chili and half the coriander leaves. Stir and fry until the onion is golden.

3 Stir in the tomato, chili powder, turmeric, coriander, fennel seeds, garam masala and half the cumin and cook over low heat, mashing the tomato with the back of a wooden spoon to make a thick paste.

4 Drain and add the vegetables with about 5 Tbsp water. Cover and cook, stirring occasionally, for about 15 minutes, until the potato is tender but not soft.

5 Meanwhile, heat the remaining butter or ghee in a separate pan and, when hot, add the remaining ground cumin. Add to the curry with the remaining coriander leaves and salt to taste.

(Photograph, see page 70)

SPICED CAULIFLOWER AND POTATO
(Aloo Gobi Masala)

INGREDIENTS (Serves 4)
1 large potato
1lb cauliflower
1 onion, chopped
1 Tbsp finely grated fresh ginger
1 tsp ground coriander
½ tsp ground cumin
1 clove garlic, finely chopped
1 tsp fennel seeds
½ tsp turmeric
½ tsp chili powder
1 tsp garam masala
leaves from 1 sprig of coriander
juice from 1 Tbsp tamarind (see page 19)
2 Tbsp oil
salt

1 Peel the potato and cut into chunks. Divide the cauliflower into florets, discarding the tough stems. Put the vegetables in a bowl of cold water to prevent discoloration.

2 In a blender or food processor, blend together the onion, ginger, ground coriander, cumin, garlic, fennel seeds, turmeric, chili powder, garam masala and coriander leaves with the tamarind juice and about 1 Tbsp water to form a thick paste.

3 Heat the oil in a pan and add the spice paste. Fry for a few minutes until the oil runs free from the spices.

4 Drain the vegetables and add to the pan with 1-2 Tbsp water. Cover and cook over low heat, stirring occasionally, for 10-15 minutes, until tender but not soft. Add salt to taste.

ABOVE Cauliflower with Potato and
Tomatoes
(Aloo Gobi Tamatar Masala)
See page 69

OPPOSITE Fried Bitter Melon
(Karela Masala)
See page 68

RED PEPPERS STUFFED WITH VEGETABLES
(Lal Mirchi Sabzi)

INGREDIENTS (Serves 4)
2 medium potatoes
¼-⅓ cup butter or ghee
1 small onion, finely chopped
1 Tbsp finely grated fresh ginger
1 clove garlic, finely chopped
½ cup peeled and chopped tomatoes
½ tsp turmeric
½ tsp chili powder
salt
½ tsp ground coriander
½ tsp garam masala
leaves from 1 sprig of coriander
4 large red peppers
2 Tbsp oil

1 Peel the potatoes, dice them and leave in a bowl of cold water to prevent discoloration.

2 Heat the butter or ghee in a pan, add the onion, ginger and garlic and fry until the onion is golden.

3 Add the tomato, turmeric, chili powder, ½ tsp salt and ground coriander, cook and stir briskly, mashing the tomato with the back of a wooden spoon to make a thick paste.

4 Drain the potato and add to the spice mix with 2-4 Tbsp water. Cover and cook over low heat, stirring occasionally, for 10-15 minutes, until the potato is tender but not soft.

5 Add the garam masala and coriander leaves. Cook for a further 3-4 minutes, then set aside, covered.

6 Wash the peppers and with a sharp knife cut off the top, which can be used as a lid. Scrape them out and discard the seeds and pith.

7 Stuff the peppers with the potato curry and replace the tops.

8 Heat the oil in a pan, put in the peppers and fry gently on all sides until cooked, about 15 minutes. Alternatively, stand the peppers in a greased dish, cover and cook in a preheated 400°F oven for 30 minutes, until tender.

(Photograph, see page 74)

GREEN PEPPERS STUFFED WITH MEAT
(*Mirchi Gosht*)

INGREDIENTS (Serves 4)
1 large potato
½ cup butter or ghee
1 small onion, finely chopped
1 Tbsp finely grated fresh ginger
2 cloves garlic, finely chopped
½ cup coarsely chopped tomatoes
½ tsp turmeric
1 tsp ground coriander
½ tsp garam masala
½ tsp fennel seeds
leaves from 1 sprig of coriander
½ tsp chili powder
1 cup lean-ground meat (beef or lamb)
1 tsp lemon juice
salt
4 large green peppers
2 Tbsp oil

1 Peel the potato, dice and leave in a bowl of cold water to prevent discoloration.

2 Heat the butter or ghee in a pan, add the onion, ginger and garlic and fry until the onion is golden.

3 Add the tomato, turmeric, ground coriander, garam masala, fennel seeds, half the coriander leaves and the chili powder and continue to fry for a few minutes until the fat runs clear of the spices.

4 Drain the potato and stir into the pan with the ground meat. Cook for 10-15 minutes, stirring occasionally, until cooked through.

5 Sprinkle with the lemon juice, add salt to taste and remove from heat.

6 Wash the peppers and with a sharp knife cut off the top, which can be used as a lid. Scrape them out and discard the seeds and pith.

7 Stuff the peppers with the curry and replace the tops.

8 Heat the oil in a pan, put in the peppers and fry gently on all sides until cooked, about 15 minutes. Alternatively, stand the peppers in a greased dish, cover and cook in a preheated 400°F oven for 30 minutes, until tender.

CARROT TORAN
(*Gajar Toran*)

INGREDIENTS (Serves 2)
2 cups peeled and diced carrots
¼ cup toor dal
salt
2 Tbsp oil
1 tsp mustard seeds
4 curry leaves
1 or 2 green chili peppers, seeded and sliced
1 cup grated fresh or dried unsweetened coconut

1 Pick over the dal, wash thoroughly and cook in water to cover for 15 minutes, until it can be crushed with the back of a wooden spoon and almost all the water has been absorbed.

2 Cook the carrots in salted water to cover for 10 minutes, until just tender. Drain and add to the dal.

3 Heat the oil in a pan and, when hot, add the mustard seeds, curry leaves and chili. Let them sizzle for a few seconds until all the seeds have popped, then add to the carrots.

4 Stir in the coconut and heat through over a low flame for 2-3 minutes, stirring, until the curry is quite dry. Add salt to taste.

GREEN PAPAYA TORAN
(*Papaya Toran*)

INGREDIENTS (Serves 2)
1lb unripe green papaya, peeled and cubed
salt
2 Tbsp oil
2 tsp polished split black lentils (urid dal)
1 small onion, finely chopped
1 tsp mustard seeds
4-6 curry leaves
1 red chili pepper, cut into 4 or 6 pieces
1⅓ cups grated fresh or dried unsweetened coconut

1 Cook the papaya in salted water to cover for 10-15 minutes, until tender but not soft. Drain and keep hot.

2 Heat the oil in a skillet and add the dal, onion, mustard seeds, curry leaves and red chili. Fry until the onion is golden, then add the papaya, stir and fry for 3-4 minutes.

3 Stir in the grated coconut and add salt to taste.

(Photograph, see page 75)

ABOVE Red Peppers Stuffed with
Vegetables
(Lal Mirchi Sabzi)
See page 72

ABOVE Green Papaya Toran
(Papaya Toran)
See page 73

BANANA KOFTA
(Kela Kofta)

INGREDIENTS (Serves 4)
4 hard green bananas
1 egg, beaten
1 Tbsp finely grated fresh ginger
1 clove garlic, finely chopped
1 green chili pepper, chopped
leaves from 1 sprig of coriander
½ cup butter or ghee
1 small onion, finely chopped
½ tsp tomato paste
½ tsp garam masala
1 tomato, peeled and chopped
½ tsp chili powder
½ tsp turmeric
1 Tbsp ground cashew nuts
1 cup yogurt
4 curry leaves
salt

1 Scrape off the tough skin of the bananas (but do not peel) and slice thickly. Cook them in about 2½ cups water for about 20 minutes, until soft.

2 Drain and mash the banana, and mix with the egg.

3 Grind or pound the ginger, garlic, green chili and half the coriander leaves, using a blender, food processor or mortar and pestle. Add to the mashed banana and mix well.

4 Form the banana mixture into small balls and set aside. Heat the butter or ghee in a pan, add the onion and remaining coriander leaves and fry until the onion is golden.

5 Add the tomato paste, garam masala and tomato and cook, mashing the tomato with the back of a wooden spoon to make a thick paste.

6 Add the chili powder, turmeric and ground cashews, then stir in the yogurt. Add 1-2 Tbsp water to thin down the sauce if desired and, when it is bubbling, add the banana balls. Simmer for 3-4 minutes, then add the curry leaves and salt to taste.

BANANA TORAN
(Kela Toran)

INGREDIENTS (Serves 2)
2 hard green bananas
salt
4 Tbsp oil
½ tsp mustard seeds
1 small onion, finely chopped
4-6 curry leaves
¼ tsp asafoetida
½ tsp ground coriander
½ tsp chili powder
½ cup peeled and chopped tomatoes

1 Scrape the bananas and cut in 2 lengthwise, then slice them and sprinkle with 1 tsp salt. Leave for 2 or 3 minutes, then rinse and dry on paper towels.

2 Heat the oil, add the mustard seeds and fry until they pop.

3 Add the onion and curry leaves and fry until the onion is golden.

4 Add the asafoetida, coriander, chili powder and tomato and cook for a further 4-5 minutes, stirring occasionally.

5 Add the banana and cook for about 15 minutes longer, until tender. Add salt to taste.

SPINACH TORAN
(Palak Toran)

INGREDIENTS (Serves 2)
1lb fresh spinach
5 Tbsp oil
1 small onion, finely chopped
1 green chili pepper, chopped
scant ½ cup peeled and chopped tomatoes
1 cup grated fresh or dried unsweetened coconut
salt

1 Wash the spinach, discard any discolored leaves and tough stems, and shake dry. Chop as finely as possible and leave in a colander to drain.

2 Heat the oil in a pan and gently fry the onion and green chili until the onion is transparent.

3 Add the spinach and tomato, cover tightly and cook over low heat for 4-5 minutes, shaking the pan occasionally, until the spinach has wilted.

4 Stir in the coconut and add salt to taste.

(Photograph, see page 78)

VEGETABLE BIRIYANI
(Sabzi Biriyani)

INGREDIENTS (Serves 4-6)

FOR THE VEGETABLES
½ tsp fennel seeds
½ tsp turmeric
seeds from 1 cardamom pod
1 inch cinnamon stick
3 cloves
1 tsp poppy seeds
2 cloves garlic, chopped
1 Tbsp grated fresh ginger
2 green chili peppers, chopped
leaves from 1 sprig of coriander
¼ cup butter or ghee
1 small onion, chopped
2 bay leaves
1 cup peeled and chopped tomatoes
⅔ cup peeled and diced carrots
2 cups peeled and diced potatoes
¾ cup fresh peas
salt

FOR THE RICE
1½-1¾ cups basmati or long grain rice
¼ cup butter or ghee
1 onion, finely chopped
1 bay leaf
½ cup cashew nuts
¼ cup ghee

1 Grind or pound the fennel seeds, turmeric, cardamom seeds, cinnamon, cloves and poppy seeds. Blend in a blender or food processor with the garlic, ginger, green chili and coriander leaves.

2 Heat the butter or ghee in a pan, add half the onion and fry until golden.

3 Add the blended spices, the bay leaves and tomato and continue to cook, mashing the tomato with the back of a wooden spoon to make a thick paste.

4 Pour in 1¼ cups water, add the carrots, potatoes, peas and ½ tsp salt and bring to a boil. Simmer for about 15 minutes, until the potatoes are cooked and the sauce is thick.

5 Meanwhile, prepare the rice. Pick over the rice, wash in 2 or 3 changes of water, then soak for 15-20 minutes (omit this step if using long grain rice). Drain thoroughly.

6 Heat the butter or ghee in a pan add the onion and crumble in the bay leaf. Fry until the onion is golden. Stir in the rice.

7 Pour in enough boiling water to cover the rice and cook, covered, for 10 minutes. Then turn off the heat and let stand, covered, for 5-10 minutes until the liquid is absorbed and the rice is tender but not soft.

8 Stir the vegetables into the rice and heat through. Add extra salt to taste.

9 Fry the cashew nuts briefly in the ghee and sprinkle over the curry.

(Photograph, see page 79)

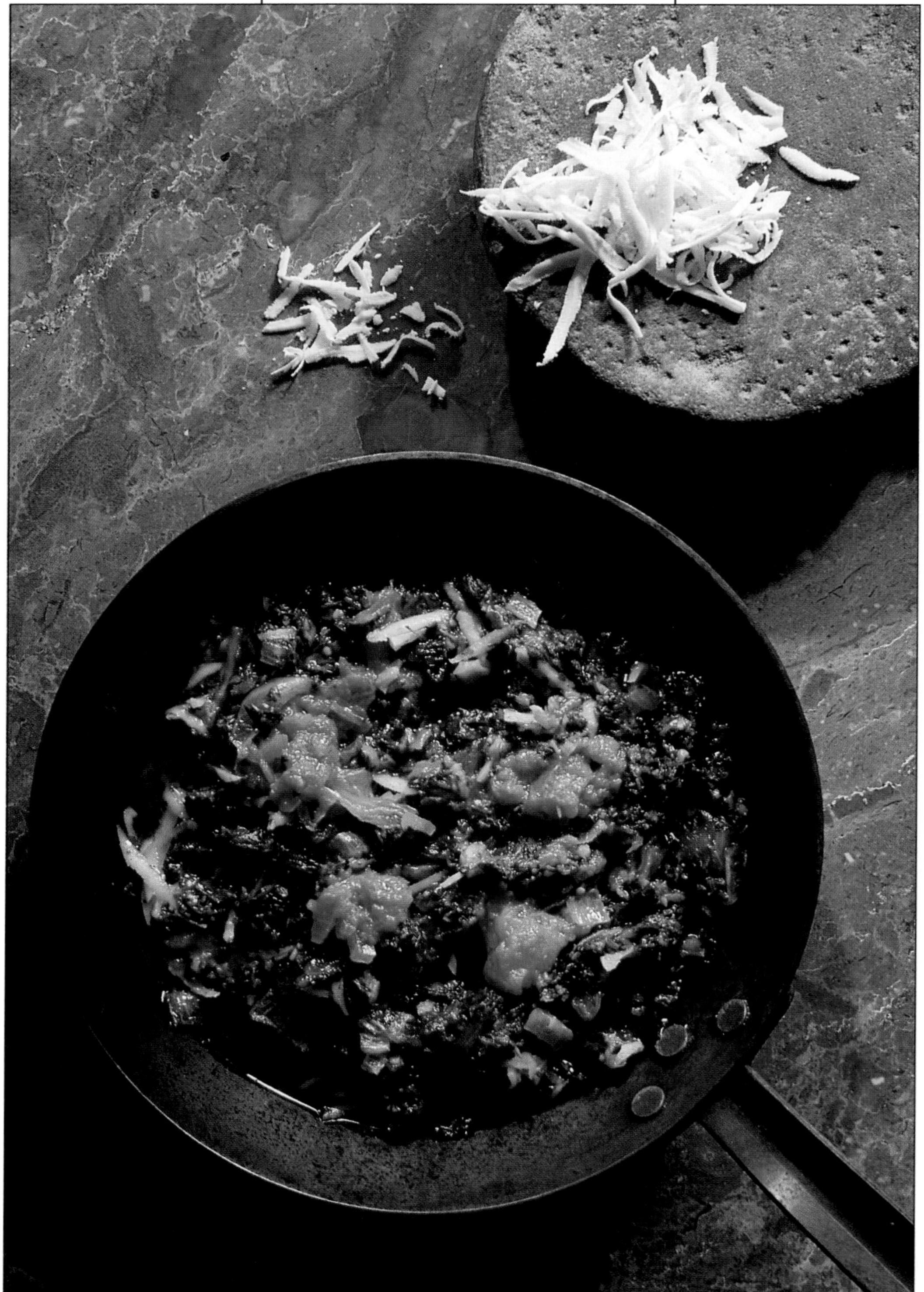

ABOVE **Vegetable Biriyani**
(Sabzi Biriyani)
See page 77
OPPOSITE **Spinach Toran**
(Palak Toran)
See page 76

MEAT DISHES
Gosht

Goat is the meat most often eaten in India, and lamb is the best substitute. Shoulder or neck are the best cuts to buy as they have more connective tissue. This means that they can be cooked for a fairly long time and end up succulent and tender.

All recipes in this section are intended for boned meat, but the bones can be left in. If you wish to do this, allow for the weight of the bones, which will be about half the total weight of the meat.

Beef and pork may also be used, although beef is not often eaten in India. For the Hindus, the cow is a sacred animal, and the Muslims are forbidden pork.

The meat you choose should be lean. Trim it carefully of any fat, gristle, etc. It is a mistake to think you can make a good curry with leftover pieces of meat. Curries involve long, slow simmering to extract the juices from the meat, so meat that has had all its juices extracted for some other purposes will not be much good.

Young, tender meat is the best to choose for kebabs, as these require faster cooking.

MEAT CURRY IN A THICK SAUCE
(Gosht Dupiaza)

INGREDIENTS (Serves 4)
1 small onion, finely chopped
2 Tbsp oil
1 Tbsp all-purpose flour
2lb meat, trimmed and cubed
1 Tbsp lemon juice
1/2 tsp ground pepper
salt
1/4 cup butter or ghee
1 cup chopped tomatoes
1 green chili pepper, sliced
leaves from 1 sprig of coriander
1/2 tsp garam masala

1 | Fry the onion in the oil until golden. Add the flour and continue to fry, stirring, until the flour is colored and has formed a paste.

2 | Add the meat, lemon juice, pepper and 1/2 tsp salt, stir and pour in about 3 3/4 cups water. Bring to a boil and simmer, covered, for about 1 hour, stirring occasionally, until the meat is tender and the sauce is thick.

3 | Heat the butter or ghee in a pan, add the tomato and green chili and fry gently, stirring, for 3-4 minutes, then add to the meat.

4 | Sprinkle on the coriander leaves and garam masala.

(Photograph, see page 83)

MEAT CURRY WITH YOGURT
(Dahi Gosht)

INGREDIENTS (Serves 4)
4-6 Tbsp oil
2 onions, coarsely chopped
2 Tbsp chopped fresh ginger
2 cloves garlic, chopped
1 green chili pepper, chopped
seeds from 2 cardamom pods
1 inch cinnamon stick
3 cloves
½ tsp fennel seeds
1 Tbsp ground coriander
1 tsp ground cumin
leaves from 2 sprigs coriander
½ tsp turmeric
1 tsp chili powder
⅔ cup yogurt
2lb meat, trimmed and cubed
4-6 curry leaves
salt

1 Heat half the oil in a pan, add half the onion, the ginger, garlic, green chili, cardamom seeds, cinnamon, cloves, fennel seeds, ground coriander, cumin, half the coriander leaves, the turmeric and chili powder and fry gently, stirring, for 10 minutes.

2 Take the pan off the heat and stir in the yogurt. Mix well and set aside.

3 Chop the remaining onion finely and fry in the remaining oil until golden. Add the meat and fry for about 15 minutes, stirring occasionally.

4 Stir in the spiced yogurt and cook gently for 8-10 minutes, stirring.

5 Pour on about 2½ cups boiling water, turn down the heat and cook, covered, for about 1 hour or until the meat is tender. Cook uncovered and stir frequently if a thicker sauce is required.

6 Sprinkle on the curry leaves and remaining coriander leaves and add salt to taste.

(Photograph, see page 82)

PLAIN MEAT CURRY
(Gosht Curry)

INGREDIENTS (Serves 4)
2lb meat, trimmed and cubed
1 Tbsp lemon juice
salt
2 Tbsp ground coriander
2 tsp chili powder
½ tsp ground pepper
1 tsp ground cumin
½ tsp turmeric
¼ cup butter or ghee
1 Tbsp oil
1 small onion, finely chopped
2 Tbsp chopped fresh ginger
2 cloves garlic, chopped
1 tsp garam masala
4-6 curry leaves

1 Wash the meat thoroughly in hot water. Drain and cook, covered, in 2½ cups fresh water with the lemon juice and a pinch of salt for about an hour or until the meat is tender and most of the liquid has evaporated.

2 Meanwhile, mix the coriander, chili powder, pepper, cumin and turmeric with 2 Tbsp water to make a smooth paste.

3 Heat the butter or ghee in a pan with the oil, add the onion, ginger and garlic and fry until the onion is golden.

4 Add the spice paste and continue to fry for 10 minutes. Add the paste to the cooked meat with ½ tsp salt and cook, covered, over low heat for 10-15 minutes, until the sauce is thick.

5 Sprinkle on the garam masala and the curry leaves and add extra salt to taste.

ABOVE Meat Curry with Yogurt
(Dahi Gosht)
See page 81

ABOVE OPPOSITE Meat Curry in a
Thick Sauce
(Gosht Dupiaza)
See page 80

BELOW OPPOSITE Meat and Tomato
Curry
(Tamatar Gosht)
See page 84

MEAT AND TOMATO CURRY
(*Tamatar Gosht*)

INGREDIENTS (Serves 4)
¼ cup butter or ghee
1 small onion, finely chopped
1 Tbsp finely grated fresh ginger
3 cloves garlic, finely chopped
1 cup peeled and chopped tomatoes
½ tsp turmeric
2 tsp chili powder
1 Tbsp ground coriander
½ tsp ground cumin
salt
1 tsp garam masala
2lb meat, trimmed and cubed
2 cups peeled and diced potatoes
leaves from 1 sprig of coriander

1. Heat the butter or ghee in a large saucepan, add the onion, ginger and garlic and fry until the onion is golden.

2. Add the tomato, turmeric, chili powder, ground coriander, cumin, ½ tsp salt and garam masala. Stir and continue to fry until the fat runs clear of the spices, then add 2½ cups boiling water and mix well.

3. Add the meat and cook, covered, over low heat for about 1 hour, until tender and the sauce is thick.

4. Add the potato and a little extra water, if necessary, and cook for a further 10-15 minutes until tender but not soft.

5. Sprinkle on the coriander leaves and extra salt to taste.

(Photograph, see page 83)

SWEET AND SOUR MEAT CURRY
(*Chuteraney*)

INGREDIENTS (Serves 4)
2 Tbsp oil
¼ cup butter or ghee
2 onions, finely chopped
1 green chili pepper, chopped
1 Tbsp finely grated fresh ginger
2 cloves garlic, crushed
1 cup peeled and chopped tomatoes
leaves from 2 sprigs of coriander
½ tsp garam masala
½ tsp turmeric
1 tsp chili powder
2lb meat, trimmed and cubed
2 cups peeled and chopped potatoes
½ tsp ground pepper
1 Tbsp sugar
⅔ cup yogurt
2 Tbsp lemon juice

1. Heat the oil and butter or ghee in a saucepan, add the onion, green chili, ginger and garlic and fry until the onion turns golden.

2. Add the tomato, half the coriander leaves, the garam masala, turmeric and chili powder and cook, stirring and mashing the tomato with the back of a wooden spoon until it makes a paste and the fat has run clear of the spices.

3. Add the meat and 2½ cups boiling water and cook over low heat for about 1 hour, until tender.

4. Add the potato and cook for a further 10-15 minutes until tender but not soft.

5. Mix the remaining coriander leaves, the pepper and sugar with the yogurt, add to the curry and cook for 2-3 minutes, stirring, to heat through.

6. Sprinkle on the lemon juice and add salt to taste.

(Photograph, see page 86)

MEAT CURRY WITH ROASTED SPICES
(Masala Gosht)

INGREDIENTS (Serves 4)
4 Tbsp oil
2 Tbsp coriander seeds
2 red chili peppers, cut into pieces
1 inch cinnamon stick
3 cloves
⅔ cup grated fresh coconut
1lb meat, trimmed and cubed
½ tsp turmeric
salt
2 green chili peppers, sliced
1 Tbsp grated fresh ginger
1 small onion, chopped
2 cups peeled and diced potatoes
1 cup peeled and chopped tomatoes
6 curry leaves

1 Heat half the oil in a pan and fry the coriander seeds, red chili, cinnamon, cloves and coconut for about 5 minutes, then transfer to a blender or mortar and reduce to a smooth paste.

2 Put the meat in a bowl with the turmeric, ½ tsp salt, green chili, ginger and half the onion, add the spice paste and mix well. Let it marinate for 15 minutes.

3 Heat the remaining oil in a large saucepan and fry the remaining onion until golden.

4 Add the marinated meat, the potato and tomato. Pour in 3¾ cups boiling water, cover and cook over low heat for about 1 hour, until the meat is tender and the sauce is thick.

5 Add extra salt to taste and sprinkle on the curry leaves.

(Photograph, see page 87)

FRIED SPICED MEAT KEEMA
(Keema Masala)

INGREDIENTS (Serves 4)
½ cup butter or ghee
1 onion, finely chopped
2 cloves garlic, finely chopped
1 Tbsp finely grated fresh ginger
leaves from 1 sprig of coriander
¾ cup peeled and chopped tomatoes
seeds from 2 cardamom pods, crushed
1 inch cinnamon stick
3 cloves
1 bay leaf
½ tsp ground coriander
½ tsp turmeric
½ tsp ground cumin
½ tsp chili powder
salt
1lb lean ground meat
2 cups peeled and diced potatoes

1 Heat the butter or ghee in a pan, add the onion and fry until golden.

2 Add the garlic, ginger, half the coriander leaves, the tomato, cardamom, cinnamon, cloves and bay leaf and fry for 3-4 minutes, stirring.

3 Add the coriander, turmeric, cumin, chili powder and ½ tsp salt and stir to make a thick paste.

4 Add the meat and potato and fry for about 15 minutes, stirring occasionally, then pour in 1¼ cups boiling water, cover and cook over low heat for a further 15 minutes, until the meat and potato are cooked and the sauce is thick.

5 Add salt to taste and sprinkle on the remaining coriander leaves.

(Photograph, see page 86)

ABOVE Sweet and Sour Meat Curry
(Chuteraney)
See page 84

ABOVE Fried Spiced Meat Keema
(Keema Masala)
See page 85

ABOVE Meat Curry with Roasted
Spices *(Masala Gosht)*
See page 85

SPICED MEAT BIRIYANI
(*Biriyani Gosht*)

INGREDIENTS (Serves 4)
²⁄₃ *cup grated fresh coconut*
½ *cup whole cashew nuts*
1 Tbsp chopped mint leaves
leaves from 2 sprigs coriander
2 Tbsp thinly sliced fresh ginger
4 cloves garlic, thinly sliced
1 green chili pepper, sliced
1 small onion, thinly sliced
²⁄₃ *cup yogurt*
1 Tbsp lemon juice
2 tsp biriyani masala
1 tsp ground coriander
salt
2lb meat, trimmed and cubed
1½ cups basmati rice, washed and soaked
   in water for 2 hours
2 Tbsp butter or ghee
2 Tbsp milk
cashew nuts, almonds and golden raisins to
   decorate

1 In a blender or food processor, blend the coconut, cashews, mint and coriander leaves to make a smooth paste. Transfer to a large bowl.

2 Stir in the ginger, garlic, green chili, onion, yogurt, lemon juice, biriyani masala, ground coriander and ½ tsp salt.

3 Turn the meat in this mixture to coat and let marinate for about 5 minutes.

4 Put the meat in a heavy-bottomed pan, pour in 2½ cups boiling water, cover and cook over low heat for about an hour, until tender.

5 Meanwhile, drain the rice and cook in 3¾ cups boiling water for 10 minutes, until half cooked. Drain.

6 In a large ovenproof casserole, heat the butter or ghee, then add the meat and rice and mix thoroughly. Cook, covered with foil or a lid, in a preheated 300°F oven for 10 minutes.

7 Sprinkle on the milk and decorate with cashews, almonds and golden raisins.

MEAT CURRY WITH NUTS AND COCONUT MILK
(*Nariel Gosht*)

INGREDIENTS (Serves 4)
flesh of 1 coconut, grated
½ *cup cashew nuts*
2 cloves garlic, chopped
½ *tsp chili powder*
1 Tbsp grated fresh ginger
½ *tsp ground coriander*
½ *tsp turmeric*
leaves from 1 sprig of coriander
½ *tsp garam masala*
½ *tsp ground pepper*
½ *cup butter or ghee*
1 small onion, chopped
2lb meat, trimmed and cubed
¼ *tsp saffron*
2 Tbsp golden raisins
½ *cup almonds*
salt
4-6 curry leaves

1 Purée the coconut in a blender or food processor with 1 Tbsp boiling water. Transfer to a square of cheesecloth and squeeze out the milk into a bowl. Return the coconut to the blender or food processor and repeat the process.

2 Grind, pound or blend in a blender or food processor the cashew nuts, garlic, chili powder, ginger, ground coriander, turmeric, coriander leaves, garam masala and pepper.

3 Heat the butter or ghee in a pan, add the onion and fry until golden, then add the blended spices and fry for a further 5 minutes.

4 Add the meat, stir and fry for 5 minutes, then add the coconut milk, saffron, golden raisins, almonds and ½ tsp salt and cook, covered, over low heat for about 1 hour, until the meat is tender and the sauce has thickened.

5 Sprinkle on the curry leaves.

(Photograph, see page 90)

MEATBALL AND CAULIFLOWER CURRY
(Phul Gobi Kofta)

not that good

INGREDIENTS (Serves 4)

FOR THE MEAT AND CAULIFLOWER
1 egg, beaten
1lb lean ground meat
1 Tbsp grated fresh ginger
2 cloves garlic, chopped
½ tsp garam masala
½ tsp ground cumin
leaves from 1 sprig of coriander
salt
1 small cauliflower, cut into florets, tough
  stems discarded

FOR THE SAUCE
⅓ cup butter or ghee
1 small onion, finely chopped
seeds from 2 cardamom pods, crushed
2 cloves
1 inch cinnamon stick
1 Tbsp grated fresh ginger
2 cloves garlic, crushed
½ tsp turmeric
1 tsp chili powder
½ tsp ground cumin
½ tsp ground coriander
1 cup peeled and chopped tomatoes or
  2 tsp tomato paste
⅔ cup yogurt
salt
leaves from 1 sprig of coriander

1 Mix the egg with the ground meat.

2 Grind, pound or purée in a blender or food processor the ginger, garlic, garam masala, cumin, coriander leaves and ½ tsp salt.

3 Mix the spice paste with the meat, form it into small balls and set aside.

4 For the sauce, heat the butter or ghee in a pan, add the onion and fry until golden.

5 Add the cardamom seeds, cloves, cinnamon, ginger, garlic, turmeric, chili powder, cumin and coriander and fry for 3 to 4 minutes, stirring.

6 Add the tomato or tomato paste and cook, stirring, until the fat runs clear of the spices.

7 Stir in the yogurt with a pinch of salt and 1-2 Tbsp water and bring gently to a boil.

8 Carefully slide in the meatballs and cauliflower florets and cook for about 20 minutes over low heat, stirring occasionally and taking care not to break the meatballs.

9 Sprinkle on the coriander leaves and add salt to taste.

(Photograph, see page 91)

ABOVE Meat Curry with Nuts and
Coconut Milk
(Nariel Gosht)
See page 88

OPPOSITE Meatball and Cauliflower
Curry
(Phul Gobi Kofta)
See page 89

MEAT KEBABS
(Seekh Kebabs)

INGREDIENTS (Serves 4)
1 Tbsp finely grated fresh ginger
1 green chili pepper, chopped
salt
½ tsp garam masala
1lb lean ground meat
1 onion, finely chopped
½ tsp chili powder
½ tsp ground pepper
½ tsp ground cumin
leaves from 1 sprig of coriander
1 egg, beaten
7 Tbsp oil

1 Grind, pound or purée in a blender or food processor the ginger, green chili, ½ tsp salt and the garam masala with 1-2 Tbsp water to make a paste.

2 In a bowl, mix the spice paste with the meat and onion, sprinkle on the chili powder, pepper, cumin and coriander leaves, add the egg and 1-2 tsp oil and combine well.

3 Roll the mixture into small sausages and thread on skewers.

4 Broil the kebabs, basting with a little oil and turning frequently until cooked through.

5 Remove the kebabs from the skewers and fry in the remaining oil for about 10 minutes, turning gently.

(Photograph, see page 95)

MEAT AND VEGETABLE CURRY
(Sabzi Gosht)

INGREDIENTS (Serves 4)
⅓ cup butter or ghee
1 small onion, finely chopped
1 Tbsp grated fresh ginger
2 cloves garlic, chopped
½ tsp turmeric
½ tsp chili powder
½ tsp ground coriander
½ tsp garam masala
½ tsp ground cumin
1 green chili pepper, chopped
4-6 curry leaves
1lb meat, trimmed and cubed
¾ cup peeled and chopped tomatoes
5 cups okra, trimmed and cut into 2 or 3 pieces
⅔ cup peeled and diced carrots
2 cups peeled and cubed potatoes
1½ cups peeled and cubed eggplant
½ cup fresh peas
salt

1 Heat the butter or ghee in a pan, add the onion and fry until golden.

2 Add the ginger, garlic, turmeric, chili powder, coriander, garam masala, cumin, green chili and curry leaves, stir and fry for a further 5 minutes.

3 Add the meat and fry for 5 minutes, then add the tomato, okra, carrot, potato, eggplant and peas, pour in 3¾ cups water, add ½ tsp salt and cook over low heat for 1 hour, until the vegetables and meat are tender and the sauce is thick.

4 Add extra salt to taste.

(Photograph, see page 95)

PORK VINDALOO
(Soor Vindaloo)

INGREDIENTS (Serves 4)
6 cloves garlic
1oz fresh ginger
4 red chili peppers, seeded
1 tsp mustard seeds
½ tsp fenugreek seeds
½ tsp turmeric
½ tsp ground cumin
5 Tbsp white wine vinegar
2-3 Tbsp oil
2 onions, finely chopped
1 cup peeled and chopped tomatoes
2lb-3lb shoulder of pork, trimmed and cubed
salt
4-6 curry leaves
6 cloves
1 inch cinnamon stick
1 tsp sugar

1 Chop 4 cloves garlic with half the ginger, then grind, pound or blend in a blender or food processor with the chilis, mustard seeds, fenugreek seeds, turmeric, cumin and half the vinegar.

2 Heat the oil, in a pan, add the onion and fry until golden.

3 Add the spice paste, stir and fry gently for 15 minutes.

4 Add the tomato and continue to cook, mashing it with the back of a wooden spoon to make a paste.

5 When the oil has run clear of the spices, add the pork and fry for 5 minutes, turning the pieces in the spice mixture.

6 Add ½ tsp salt and pour in 2½ cups boiling water. Simmer, covered, for 40 minutes, until the pork is tender.

7 Slice the remaining garlic and ginger and add with the curry leaves, cloves and cinnamon stick. Cook for a further 5 minutes.

8 Add the sugar and remaining vinegar. Add salt to taste.

OPPOSITE Meat Kebabs
(Seekh Kebabs)
See page 92

RIGHT Meat and Vegetable Curry
(Sabzi Gosht)
See page 92

BELOW Pork Vindaloo
(Soor Vindaloo)
See page 93

CHICKEN DISHES
Murghi

In India chicken used to be a special treat and many spectacular and elegant dishes were devised to make the most of it. Today, however, it makes quite a regular appearance at the tables of meat-eating families.

Older birds have more flavor and these can be used in dishes requiring long, slow cooking, which will tenderize the flesh. Quicker-cooking dishes call for young birds that are tender in the first place.

Overcooking chicken ruins it — it gets dehydrated, tough and stringy, unlike red meat — and so testing is important. Stick a skewer into the thickest part of the meat, or at a joint, and if the juices run clear and the flesh is white, the meat is done. Chicken should be basted frequently to keep it from drying out and to seal in its natural juices.

You can use chicken parts for most of the recipes in this section, or buy a whole bird and cut it up into smaller pieces yourself. Indians usually skin chicken before cooking it to allow the aromatics to permeate the meat.

CHICKEN BIRIYANI
(Murghi Biriyani)

INGREDIENTS (Serves 4-6)

FOR THE CHICKEN
1 Tbsp biriyani masala
1 green chili pepper
1 Tbsp finely grated fresh ginger
2 cloves garlic, chopped
leaves from 2 sprigs coriander
1 Tbsp chopped mint leaves
½ cup cashew nuts
3lb chicken
7 Tbsp oil
¼ cup butter or ghee
1 small onion, chopped
1 cup peeled and chopped tomatoes
salt

FOR THE RICE
½ cup butter or ghee
2 bay leaves
1 small onion, chopped
generous 1 cup basmati rice , washed, soaked
    in water for 20 minutes and drained
10 cashew nuts
⅓ cup golden raisins

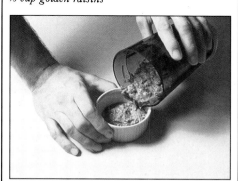

1 Pound, grind or purée in a blender or food processor the biriyani masala, green chili, ginger, garlic, coriander leaves, mint and cashews, adding about 2 Tbsp water to make a paste.

2 Skin the chicken and cut into 8 pieces. Wash in hot water and dry on paper towels.

3 Heat 5 Tbsp oil in a pan, add the chicken and fry for about 10 minutes, turning once. Remove the chicken.

4 Add the remaining oil and the butter or ghee to the pan and, when hot, add the onion and fry until golden.

5 Add the spice mixture and cook, stirring, until the fat runs clear of the spices.

6 Add the tomato, mashing it with the back of a wooden spoon to make a paste.

7 Add the chicken pieces and salt and pour in 2½ cups boiling water. Cook for about 1 hour, until the chicken is tender and the sauce has thickened.

8 Meanwhile, for the rice, heat three-quarters of the butter or ghee in a heavy-bottomed saucepan, add the bay leaves and onion and fry until the onion is golden.

9 Pour in the rice and stir well over low heat for about 10 minutes, until the rice is translucent.

10 Add 2½ cups boiling water, bring back to a boil and cook over low heat, covered, for 8-10 minutes. Drain off the water.

11 Mix the rice, chicken and sauce together in an ovenproof casserole, cover with a lid or foil and cook in a preheated 300°F oven for 10-15 minutes, until the rice is completely cooked. This dish should be moist but not too wet.

12 Fry the cashews and golden raisins briefly in the remaining butter or ghee and sprinkle on top of the curry.

(Photograph, see page 99)

CHICKEN WITH HONEY
(Murghi Madh)

INGREDIENTS (Serves 4)
1 Tbsp finely grated fresh ginger
2 cloves garlic, crushed
2 Tbsp lemon juice
5 Tbsp honey
1 Tbsp paprika
1 tsp chili powder
1 Tbsp cornstarch
½ tsp salt
8 chicken legs
¼ cup butter or ghee
1 Tbsp lemon juice
leaves from 1-2 sprigs coriander

1 Combine the ginger and the next 7 ingredients in a mortar, blender or food processor and pound or purée well to make a smooth paste.

2 Wash the chicken pieces, dry them on paper towels and prick them all over with the point of a sharp knife.

3 Rub the spice paste all over the chicken and let stand for at least 20 minutes to marinate.

4 Lay the chicken pieces on a rack across a roasting pan and cook in a preheated 400°F oven for 45 minutes until the meat is cooked through.

5 Sprinkle with the lemon juice and garnish with coriander leaves.

(Photograph, see page 98)

ABOVE Chicken with Honey
(Murghi Madh)
See page 97

OPPOSITE Chicken Biriyani
(Murghi Biriyani)
See page 96

CHICKEN WITH SPICES
(Murghi Masala)

INGREDIENTS (Serves 4)
2-3 Tbsp oil
2 cloves garlic, chopped
1 Tbsp finely grated fresh ginger
leaves from 1 sprig of coriander
½ tsp garam masala
1 tsp ground coriander
1 tsp ground cumin
4 cashew nuts
1 Tbsp paprika
1 tsp chili powder
1 Tbsp lemon juice
1-2 tsp salt
8 chicken legs
⅔ cup yogurt

1 In a blender or food processor, blend all the ingredients except the chicken and yogurt to a thick paste, then stir in the yogurt and mix thoroughly.

2 Wash the chicken pieces, dry on paper towels and prick all over with the point of a sharp knife.

3 Smother the chicken in the spice paste and marinate for about 3 hours.

4 Lay the chicken pieces on a rack across a roasting pan and cook in a preheated 400°F oven for 45 minutes until the chicken is tender.

5 Sprinkle with extra salt to taste.

(Photograph, see page 102)

CHICKEN, TANDOORI STYLE
(Murghi Tandoori)

INGREDIENTS (Serves 4)
8 chicken legs
1-2 Tbsp lemon juice
salt
1 Tbsp finely grated fresh ginger
3 cloves garlic, chopped
1 tsp ground coriander
½ tsp ground cumin
1 tsp chili powder
2 Tbsp paprika
red food coloring (optional)
1 tsp garam masala
½ tsp ground black pepper
⅔ cup yogurt
1 lemon, sliced
1 small onion, sliced

1 Skin the chicken legs, wash thoroughly and dry on paper towels. Slash them with a sharp pointed knife.

2 Rub in the lemon juice and sprinkle with salt.

3 Blend the ginger and garlic in a blender or food processor with 1 Tbsp water, then mix with the coriander, cumin, chili powder, paprika, red food coloring, garam masala and pepper and stir into the yogurt.

4 Smother the chicken legs in the spiced yogurt and refrigerate, covered, to marinate overnight.

5 Lay the chicken legs on a rack across a roasting pan and cook in a preheated 400°F oven for about 45 minutes, until tender.

6 Sprinkle with extra salt to taste and garnish with lemon and onion slices.

(Photograph, see page 103)

CHICKEN AND TOMATO CURRY (*Tamatar aur Murghi*)

INGREDIENTS (Serves 4)
generous ½ cup butter or ghee
2 onions, chopped
3 cloves garlic, crushed
1 Tbsp finely grated fresh ginger
1 green chili pepper, chopped
seeds from 2 cardamom pods, crushed
3 cloves
1 inch cinnamon stick
1 bay leaf
1 cup peeled and chopped tomatoes
½ tsp turmeric
½ tsp chili powder
½ tsp paprika
1 Tbsp ground coriander
½ tsp fennel seeds
1 chicken, about 3lb, skinned and cut into
    pieces
2 cups peeled and diced potatoes
¼ tsp ground pepper
¼ tsp saffron
salt
leaves from 2 sprigs of coriander

1 Heat the butter or ghee in a pan, add the onion, garlic, ginger, green chili, cardamom seeds, cloves, cinnamon and bay leaf and fry until the onion is golden.

2 Add the tomato and continue to cook, mashing it with the back of a wooden spoon to make a paste.

3 Add the turmeric, chili powder, paprika, ground coriander and fennel seeds and fry until the fat runs clear of the spices.

4 Add the chicken pieces and fry for 5 minutes, then pour in 3¾ cups boiling water, add the potato and cook over low heat, covered, for 1 hour, until the chicken is cooked and the sauce has thickened.

5 Sprinkle on the pepper, saffron, salt and coriander leaves.

(Photograph, see page 102)

PLAIN CHICKEN CURRY (*Sada Murghi*)

INGREDIENTS (Serves 4)
½ tsp turmeric
½ tsp chili powder
2 tsp ground coriander
4 Tbsp oil
1 onion, finely chopped
½ tsp ground pepper
3 cloves garlic, crushed
1 Tbsp finely grated fresh ginger
1 cup peeled and chopped tomatoes
¼ cup butter or ghee
3lb chicken, skinned and cut into pieces
¼ tsp saffron
2-3 tsp sugar
salt
leaves from 1 sprig of coriander

1 Mix the turmeric, chili powder and ground coriander with 2 Tbsp water.

2 Heat the oil in a pan, add the onion and fry until golden.

3 Add the pepper, garlic and ginger, fry for 3-4 minutes until the fragrance emerges, then add the tomato and the spice paste and continue to fry until the oil runs clear of the spices.

4 Add the butter or ghee and when melted, add the chicken pieces and 3¾ cups boiling water and cook over low heat for about 1 hour, until the chicken is tender.

5 Sprinkle on the saffron, sugar, salt to taste and coriander leaves.

ABOVE Chicken with Spices
(Murghi Masala)
See page 100

LEFT Chicken and Tomato Curry
(Tamatar aur Murghi)
See page 101

ABOVE Chicken, Tandoori Style
(Murghi Tandoori)
See page 100

CHICKEN CURRY WITH YOGURT
(Murghi Dahi)

INGREDIENTS (Serves 4)
5 Tbsp oil
2 onions, finely chopped
2 cloves garlic, finely chopped
1 Tbsp finely grated fresh ginger
seeds from 2 cardamom pods
1 inch cinnamon stick
2 cloves
½ tsp fennel seeds
1 tsp paprika
2 tsp ground coriander
½ tsp ground cumin
½ tsp chili powder
½ tsp turmeric
⅔ cup yogurt
3lb chicken, skinned and cut into pieces
2 cups peeled and diced potatoes
1 cup peeled and chopped tomatoes
salt
leaves from 2 sprigs of coriander

1 Heat 4 Tbsp oil in a pan, add the onion, garlic, ginger, cardamom seeds, cinnamon, cloves and fennel seeds and fry until the onion is golden.

2 Add the paprika, ground coriander, cumin, chili powder and turmeric and continue to fry until the oil runs free from the spice mixture.

3 Drain off the oil, stir in the yogurt and purée in a blender or food processor until smooth.

4 Fry the remaining onion in the remaining oil until golden, add the chicken and continue to fry for 5 minutes.

5 Add the blended spice mixture, the potato, tomato, ½ tsp salt and 3¾ cups boiling water and cook over low heat for about 1 hour, until the meat and vegetables are done.

6 Add extra salt to taste and sprinkle with the coriander leaves.

(Photograph, see page 107)

CHICKEN KEBABS
(Murghi Kebabs)

INGREDIENTS (Serves 2)
2 Tbsp soy sauce
2 Tbsp oil
1 tsp ground black pepper
1lb boned chicken, skinned and cubed

1 Mix the soy sauce, oil and pepper with 1 Tbsp water, pour over the chicken, turn to coat and let marinate for at least an hour.

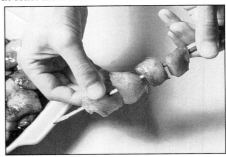

2 Thread the chicken cubes onto skewers and broil slowly for 25-30 minutes, turning and basting occasionally with the marinade, until cooked through.

(Photograph, see page 106)

WHOLE ROAST CHICKEN
(Murghi Masala)

INGREDIENTS (Serves 4)
1 chicken, about 3lb, skinned
½ tsp ground black pepper
salt
½ cup ground almonds
2 Tbsp finely grated fresh ginger
2 cloves garlic, chopped
leaves from 2 sprigs of coriander
1 onion, finely chopped
1 tsp garam masala
1 tsp paprika
1 tsp chili powder
1 tsp ground coriander
¼ tsp saffron
1 tsp ground cumin
⅔ cup yogurt
1 Tbsp lemon juice

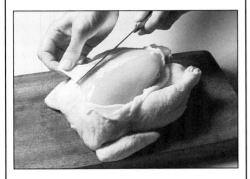

1 Skin and wash the chicken and dry with paper towels. Prick all over with a sharp knife, rub in the black pepper and ½ tsp salt and let stand to absorb the flavors for about 30 minutes.

2 Pound, grind or blend in a blender or food processor the almonds, ginger, garlic, coriander leaves, onion, garam masala, paprika, chili powder, ground coriander, saffron and cumin, then mix well with the yogurt.

3 Smother the chicken in the spiced yogurt and marinate for at least 4 hours.

4 Put the chicken in a roasting pan and cook in a preheated 400°F oven, basting occasionally, for up to 2 hours, until chicken is tender and the juices run clear when the bird is pierced with a skewer.

5 Sprinkle with lemon juice and salt to taste.

(Photograph, see page 107)

SPICED CHICKEN
(Murghi Masala)

INGREDIENTS (Serves 4)
3 Tbsp coriander seeds
2 red chili peppers, cut into 3 or 4 pieces
1 inch cinnamon stick
2 cloves
⅔ cup grated fresh coconut
½ tsp turmeric
2 onions, finely chopped
1 Tbsp finely grated fresh ginger
4-6 curry leaves
2lb chicken parts, skinned
4 Tbsp oil
2 green chili peppers, seeded and cut into 3 or 4 pieces
2 bay leaves
½ cup peeled and chopped tomatoes
salt

1 Heat a pan without any fat or oil until very hot, then add the coriander seeds, red chili, cinnamon stick and cloves and roast them for 5-6 minutes, shaking the pan to prevent them from burning. Grind or pound the roasted spices into a fine powder.

2 Blend the spices and coconut together in a blender or food processor. Transfer to a bowl.

3 Stir in the turmeric, three-quarters of the onion, the ginger and half the curry leaves.

4 Smother the chicken with the spice mixture and let marinate for 10-15 minutes.

5 Heat the oil in a pan and add the remaining onion, green chili and bay leaves. Fry until the onion is golden.

6 Add about 3¾ cups water, the tomato and chicken pieces and cook gently, covered, for an hour, until the chicken is tender and the sauce is thick.

7 Add salt to taste.

OPPOSITE Chicken Kebabs
(Murghi Kebabs)
See page 104

ABOVE Chicken Curry with
Yogurt
(Murghi Dahi)
See page 104

RIGHT Whole Roast Chicken
(Murghi Masala)
See page 105

FISH & SHRIMP
Machi aur Jhinga

There are said to be over 2,000 varieties of fish and shellfish available in India. They form an important part of the diet, especially for non-meat eaters. The cold-water fish that swim in the seas around Europe and America are not natives to the warm waters of the Indian Ocean, but they are equally suited to Indian cooking. Best varieties are the firm-fleshed white fish such as cod, haddock or halibut.

In India, fish are poached, steamed, baked or fried. Fish in batter is very popular: the batter absorbs flavors from the oil as well as keeping the natural flavors of the fish sealed in. Indians enjoy fish barbecued over fragrant wood or wrapped in banana leaves and cooked in the embers of the fire.

When buying fish, always make sure it is very fresh. It should never smell fishy. Use frozen shrimp in these recipes if you are unable to get fresh ones.

FISH CURRY
(Machi Kalia)

INGREDIENTS (Serves 2)
1lb white fish, boned and skinned
5 Tbsp oil
1 onion, finely chopped
½ tsp fennel seeds
⅔ cup grated fresh coconut
1 tsp chili powder
¼ tsp turmeric
4 Tbsp tamarind juice (see page 19)
1 Tbsp finely grated fresh ginger
¼ cup peeled and chopped tomatoes
1 green chili pepper, chopped
salt
4-6 curry leaves

1 Cut the fish into 2 inch squares and wash well.

2 Heat 4 Tbsp oil in a pan, add three-quarters of the onion, the fennel seeds and coconut and fry until the onion is golden.

3 Add the chili powder and turmeric and continue to cook for 4-5 minutes, then pound, grind or blend in a blender or food processor.

4 Heat the tamarind juice in a small saucepan over low heat and mix in the blended spices, ginger, tomato and green chili.

5 Heat until the mixture bubbles, then add the fish and ½ tsp salt and cook gently for 10 minutes, until the fish is tender.

6 Meanwhile, fry the remaining onion in the remaining oil until golden. Add to the curry when the fish is cooked.

7 Sprinkle on the curry leaves and add extra salt to taste.

(Photograph, see page 110)

FISH MOLIE
(*Mouli*)

INGREDIENTS (Serves 2)
1lb white fish, boned and skinned
salt
flesh of 1 coconut, grated
4 Tbsp oil
1 onion, finely chopped
1 Tbsp finely grated fresh ginger
2 green chili peppers, chopped
¼ tsp turmeric
2 tsp ground coriander
1 tsp cornstarch
2 Tbsp white wine vinegar
4-6 curry leaves

1 Rub the fish with salt, let stand for 5 minutes and then rinse under cold running water. Cut into large chunks and set aside.

2 Blend the coconut in a blender or food processor with 1-2 Tbsp boiling water. Transfer to a square of cheesecloth and squeeze the milk into a bowl. Return the coconut to the blender and repeat the process.

3 Heat the oil in a pan, add the onion, ginger, green chili, turmeric and coriander and fry until the onion is golden.

4 Mix the cornstarch with the coconut milk, add to the pan and bring to a boil.

5 Add the fish and ½ tsp salt and cook gently for 10 minutes, until the fish is tender.

6 Add the vinegar, cook for a further minute, then take the curry from the heat and sprinkle on the curry leaves.

(Photograph, see page 111)

CHILI FRIED SHRIMP
(*Jhinga Lal Mirchi*)

INGREDIENTS (Serves 2)
1⅓ cups shelled shrimp
½ tsp turmeric
1 tsp chili powder
salt
2 Tbsp oil
1 lemon, sliced, for garnish

1 Wash the shrimp well and dry them on paper towels.

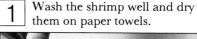

2 Mix them with the turmeric, chili powder and ½ tsp salt in a bowl, and let marinate for 10 minutes.

3 Heat the oil in a pan, add the shrimp and fry gently for 5 minutes.

4 Transfer the shrimp to a serving dish and decorate with lemon slices.

(Photograph, see page 111)

ABOVE Fish Curry
(Machi Kalia)
See page 108

OPPOSITE ABOVE Fish Molie
(Mouli)
See page 109

OPPOSITE BELOW Chili Fried Shrimp
(Jhinga Lal Mirchi)
See page 109

SARDINES IN A THICK SPICY SAUCE
(*Machli Curry*)

INGREDIENTS (*Serves 4*)
4 Tbsp oil
2 Tbsp coriander seeds
3 red chili peppers, cut into pieces
²/₃-1 cup grated fresh coconut
1-2 Tbsp tamarind juice (see page 19)
1 green chili pepper, chopped
1 Tbsp finely grated fresh ginger
1 onion, finely chopped
¼ tsp turmeric
1lb fresh sardines, cleaned
salt
4-6 curry leaves

| 1 | Heat half the oil in a pan, add the coriander seeds and red chili and fry for 3-4 minutes until the fragrance emerges, then grind, pound or blend with the coconut.

| 2 | Return to the pan and continue to fry, adding the tamarind, green chili, ginger, half the onion and the turmeric, for a further 5-7 minutes, until they make a thick paste.

| 3 | Lay the sardines on a plate, smother them in the paste and let marinate for 15 minutes.

| 4 | Meanwhile, heat the remaining oil and fry the remaining onion until golden.

| 5 | Add the marinated sardines to the pan with 2 Tbsp water, cover and cook over low heat for 5-8 minutes, until tender.

| 6 | Add salt to taste and sprinkle on the curry leaves.

(Photograph, see page 115)

SHRIMP BIRIYANI
(*Jhinga Biriyani*)

INGREDIENTS (*Serves 4*)

FOR THE SHRIMP
1 green chili pepper
1 Tbsp finely grated fresh ginger
1 clove garlic, chopped
²/₃ cup grated fresh or dried unsweetened
    coconut
4 cashew nuts
2 tsp biriyani masala
¼ cup butter or ghee
1 small onion, chopped
1lb shelled shrimp
salt
1 Tbsp lemon juice
cashew nuts and golden raisins, fried in a little
    butter or ghee, for decoration

FOR THE RICE
¼ cup butter or ghee
1 small onion, chopped
2 bay leaves
generous 1 cup basmati rice , washed, soaked
    in water for 20 minutes and drained
salt
1 cup fresh peas

| 1 | Grind, pound or blend in a blender or food processor the chili, ginger, garlic, coconut, cashews and biriyani masala to make a thick paste.

| 2 | Heat the butter or ghee in a pan, add the onion and fry until golden.

3 Add the blended spice paste and fry for a further 5-8 minutes, stirring.

4 Add the shrimp and ½ tsp salt and cook over low heat for 3-4 minutes, stirring, until the shrimp are heated through and coated in the spice mixture.

5 For the rice, heat the butter or ghee in another pan, add the onion and bay leaves and fry until the onion turns golden.

6 Pour in the rice, stir and fry for about 10 minutes, until translucent.

7 Add ½ tsp salt, the peas and enough water to cover and simmer over low heat for 10-15 minutes, until the rice is almost cooked.

8 Stir the shrimp and rice together in an ovenproof casserole, cover with a lid or foil and cook in a preheated 300°F oven 10-15 minutes.

9 Sprinkle with the lemon juice, cashews and golden raisins and add extra salt to taste.

(Photograph, see page 114)

FISH CURRY WITH YOGURT (*Dahi Machi*)

INGREDIENTS (Serves 2)
4 Tbsp oil
6 cloves garlic, finely chopped
½ tsp fenugreek seeds
1 onion, finely chopped
2 tsp chili powder
1 tsp ground coriander
salt
1lb white fish, boned, skinned and cubed
1 cup peeled and chopped tomatoes
⅔ cup yogurt
4-6 curry leaves

1 Heat the oil in a pan, add the garlic and fry until golden.

2 Add the fenugreek seeds and continue to cook until lightly browned. Remove garlic and fenugreek with a slotted spoon and set aside.

3 Add the onion to the pan and fry until golden, then return the garlic and fenugreek to the pan and cook for a further 3-4 minutes.

4 Add the chili powder and coriander and cook for 3-4 minutes until their fragrance emerges.

5 Pour in about 1¼ cups water and bring to a boil. Add ½ tsp salt, then add the fish and tomato and cook gently for 10-15 minutes, until the fish is tender and the sauce is thick.

6 Stir in the yogurt and curry leaves, taking care not to break up the fish. Heat through for 2-3 minutes and then add extra salt to taste.

(Photograph, see page 114)

ABOVE Fish Curry with Yogurt
(Dahi Machi)
See page 113

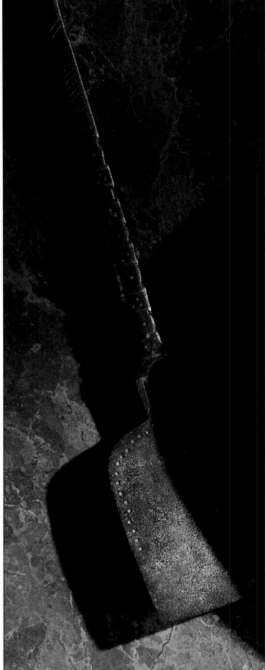

ABOVE Shrimp Biriyani
(Jhinga Biriyani)
See page 112

ABOVE Sardines in a Thick Spicy
Sauce *(Machli Curry)*
See page 112

FRIED SPICED FISH
(Machi Masala)

INGREDIENTS (Serves 2)
1 onion, finely chopped
1 Tbsp finely grated fresh ginger
6 curry leaves
salt
¼ tsp turmeric
1 tsp chili powder
1lb white fish, boned, skinned and cubed
5 Tbsp oil

1 Pound, grind or blend in a blender or food processor the onion, ginger, curry leaves, ½ tsp salt, the turmeric and chili powder .

2 Spread the paste over the fish and let marinate for about 2 hours.

3 Heat the oil in a large pan that will hold the fish in one layer, add the fish and fry for about 10 minutes, until tender.

4 Add extra salt to taste.

(Photograph, see page 118)

BAKED FISH STUFFED WITH MUSHROOMS
(Kumban Machi)

INGREDIENTS (Serves 4)
4 Tbsp oil
1 onion, sliced and separated into rings
1 Tbsp finely grated fresh ginger
1 tsp chopped mint leaves
1 cup peeled and chopped tomatoes
½ tsp chili powder
salt
2½ cups sliced mushrooms
1-1½lb whole fish, such as cod, cleaned
2 Tbsp lemon juice

1 Heat 2 Tbsp oil in a pan, add the onion, ginger and mint and fry until the onion is golden.

2 Add the tomato, chili powder and ½ tsp salt and cook, mashing the tomato into a thick paste with the back of a wooden spoon.

3 Add the mushrooms and continue to cook for 6-7 minutes.

4 Use this mixture to stuff the fish. Lay it in a greased ovenproof dish, sprinkle with the remaining oil and the lemon juice, cover with foil and bake in a preheated 350°F oven 30-35 minutes, until tender.

5 Remove skin and serve.

(Photograph, see page 118)

FRIED SPICED SHRIMP
(*Jhinga Masala*)

INGREDIENTS (Serves 2)
2 tsp ground coriander
1 tsp chili powder
½ tsp turmeric
⅔-1 cup grated fresh coconut
½ cup peeled and chopped tomatoes
1 onion, finely chopped
1 Tbsp finely grated fresh ginger
salt
1⅓ cups shelled shrimp
5 Tbsp oil
4-6 curry leaves
1 Tbsp lemon juice
leaves from 1 sprig of coriander

1 Grind, pound or blend the ground coriander, chili powder, turmeric and coconut.

2 Mix with the tomato, half the onion, the ginger and ½ tsp salt. Coat the shrimp in this mixture and let marinate for 10-15 minutes.

3 Heat the oil in a pan, add the remaining onion and the curry leaves and fry until the onion is golden.

4 Add the shrimp and cook gently for 10 minutes.

5 Remove curry from the heat, add extra salt to taste and sprinkle with the lemon juice and coriander leaves.

(Photograph, see page 119)

SHRIMP VINDALOO
(*Jhinga Vindaloo*)

INGREDIENTS (Serves 4)
½ tsp cumin seeds
2 Tbsp finely grated fresh ginger
1-2 cloves garlic, finely chopped
1 tsp mustard seeds
4 Tbsp oil
2 onions, finely chopped
6 curry leaves
½ cup peeled and chopped tomatoes
2 tsp chili powder
½ tsp turmeric
1lb shelled jumbo shrimp (or crawfish)
4 Tbsp white wine vinegar
1 tsp cornstarch, optional
salt
½ tsp sugar, optional

1 Crush the cumin seeds with the ginger, garlic and mustard seeds.

2 Heat the oil in a pan, add the onion and curry leaves and fry until the onion is golden.

3 Add the tomato, chili powder, turmeric and 1-2 Tbsp water and cook, mashing the tomato with the back of a wooden spoon to make a thick paste.

4 Add the crushed spices and continue to fry for 5 minutes, then add the shrimp and 5 Tbsp water and simmer for 10 minutes.

5 Pour in the vinegar. The sauce may be thickened, if necessary, by adding the cornstarch mixed with 1 tsp water. Add salt to taste and sugar, if desired.

(Photograph, see page 119)

ABOVE Baked Fish Stuffed with
Mushrooms
(Kumban Machi)
See page 116

LEFT Fried Spiced Fish
(Machi Masala)
See page 116

ABOVE OPPOSITE Fried Spiced
Shrimp
(Jhinga Masala)
See page 117

BELOW OPPOSITE Shrimp Vindaloo
(Jhinga Vindaloo)
See page 117

EGGS

Unday

Eggs can be used to make a very quick and satisfying curry. Hard-cooked eggs can be shelled and pierced with the point of a sharp knife to let in the flavors of the sauce they are being cooked in. Curried scrambled eggs make a very speedy lunch for one, as well as an unusual side dish at dinner.

YELLOW RICE WITH HARD-COOKED EGGS
(Unday Ki Biriyani)

INGREDIENTS (Serves 4-6)
1½-1¾ cups basmati rice
½ cup butter or ghee
1 small onion, chopped
2 cloves garlic, chopped
1 green chili pepper, chopped
seeds from 2 cardamom pods
2 bay leaves
3 cloves
salt
½ tsp turmeric
1 chicken bouillon cube, optional
10-15 cashew nuts
¼ cup ghee
2 Tbsp golden raisins
4-6 hard-cooked eggs
1 tsp lemon juice

1 | Wash the rice thoroughly in 2 or 3 changes of water, then soak for 10-15 minutes.

2 | Heat the butter or ghee in a saucepan, add the onion, garlic, green chili, cardamom seeds, bay leaves and cloves, and fry until the onion is golden.

3 | Drain the rice, pour it into the saucepan, stir and fry for 10 minutes, until it turns translucent.

4 | Pour in 2½ cups boiling water, add ½ tsp salt, the turmeric and the bouillon cube, and simmer over low heat for 10 minutes. Turn off heat and let stand, covered, for 5 minutes until all the moisture has been absorbed and the grains of rice are separate and tender.

(Photograph, see page 122)

5 Fry the cashew nuts for a couple of minutes in the ghee, adding the golden raisins for the last few seconds.

6 Cut the eggs in half, sprinkle with lemon juice and rub with salt.

7 Spread the rice in a serving dish, sprinkle with salt to taste and arrange the eggs, cashew nuts and golden raisins on top.

CURRIED EGGS
(*Unday Ki*)

INGREDIENTS (Serves 4-6)
3-4 Tbsp oil
2 small onions, grated
1 Tbsp finely grated fresh ginger
2 cloves garlic, crushed
1 inch cinnamon stick
1 bay leaf
½ tsp chili powder
2 Tbsp ground coriander
2 cashew nuts, ground
1 cup peeled and chopped tomatoes
salt
6 hard-cooked eggs
½ tsp garam masala
leaves from 1 sprig of coriander
1 tsp lemon juice
4 peppercorns, crushed

1 Heat the oil in a pan, add the onion, ginger, garlic, cinnamon and bay leaf and fry until the onion is golden.

2 Add the chili powder, ground coriander, cashews and tomato and continue to cook, mashing the tomato with the back of a wooden spoon to make a thick paste.

3 Pour in ⅔ cup water with ½ tsp salt, bring to a boil and add the eggs. Cook over low heat for 5 minutes.

4 Take the curry off the heat and sprinkle on the garam masala, coriander leaves, lemon juice and pepper. Add extra salt to taste.

(Photograph, see page 123)

ABOVE Yellow Rice with
Hard-Cooked Eggs
(Unday Ki Biriyani)
See page 120

ABOVE **Curried Eggs**
(Unday Ki)
See page 121

WHOLE EGGS FRIED WITH SPICE
(*Unday Masala*)

INGREDIENTS (Serves 4-6)
6 hard-cooked eggs
2 Tbsp oil
2 tsp ground coriander
1 tsp chili powder
¼ tsp ground pepper
salt
2 Tbsp lemon juice

1 Make several cuts into the eggs with the point of a sharp knife to allow the spices to enter.

2 Heat the oil in a pan, add the coriander, chili powder, pepper and salt and fry for about 3 minutes.

3 Add the lemon juice and stir to make a paste.

4 Add the eggs to the pan and turn in the paste to coat. Continue cooking, turning occasionally, for 4-5 minutes.

(Photograph, see page 126)

SCRAMBLED EGGS WITH ONION
(*Piyaz Ekuri*)

INGREDIENTS (Serves 2)
1 small onion, finely chopped
1 tsp chili powder
2 curry leaves
2 eggs, beaten
salt
1-2 Tbsp oil

1 Pound, grind, or blend in a blender or food processor the onion, chili powder and curry leaves, then mix with the beaten egg and ½ tsp salt.

2 Heat the oil in a pan, add the eggs and cook gently, stirring, until scrambled, about 2 minutes. (The eggs will continue to cook after you have removed them from the heat, so be careful not to overcook.)

SPICED SCRAMBLED EGG (*Ekuri*)

INGREDIENTS (Serves 2)
2 eggs
1 small onion, finely chopped
1 green chili pepper, finely chopped
2 curry leaves
1 Tbsp finely grated fresh ginger
2 Tbsp oil
salt

1 Beat the eggs well.

2 Stir together the onion, chili, curry leaves and ginger.

3 Heat the oil in a pan, add the onion mixture and fry for 3 minutes, stirring.

4 Add the egg and cook gently, stirring, for about 2 minutes, until scrambled. (The egg will continue cooking after you take it from the heat, so be careful not to overcook.) Add salt to taste.

SCRAMBLED EGGS WITH MUSHROOMS AND SHRIMP (*Jhinga Kumban Ekuri*)

INGREDIENTS (Serves 2)
2 Tbsp oil
1 small onion, finely chopped
¾ cup sliced mushrooms
½ cup shelled shrimp
1 Tbsp finely grated fresh ginger
1 green chili pepper, finely chopped
scant ½ cup peeled and chopped tomatoes
2 curry leaves
3 eggs, beaten
salt

1 Heat the oil in a pan, add the onion and fry until golden.

2 Add the mushrooms, shrimp, ginger, green chili, tomato and curry leaves and fry, stirring, for 5 minutes.

3 Add the egg with ½ tsp salt and cook gently, stirring, for about 3 minutes to scramble. (The egg will continue to cook after you take it from the heat, so be careful not to overcook.)

(Photograph, see page 127)

ABOVE Whole Eggs Fried with
Spice
(Unday Masala)
See page 124

ABOVE Scramble Eggs with
Mushrooms and Shrimp
(*Jhinga Kumban Ekuri*)
See page 125

BREADS
Roti

Indian bread is flat, unleavened bread best eaten a few minutes after cooking. If you have an Indian grocer nearby, you will be able to buy chapathi flour or ata — refined flour which, in many homes in India, is ground by hand. Otherwise wholewheat flour is a good substitute.

Breads are deep-fried or cooked on a hot *tava* or flat pan, without any oil or fat, until they puff up and are speckled brown.

Stuffed bread (see page 129) can make a meal on its own with a vegetable curry and some chutney.

WHOLEWHEAT UNLEAVENED BREAD
(Chapathis)

INGREDIENTS (Serves 4-6)
2 cups wholewheat flour
½ tsp salt
boiling water

1 Sift the flour into a bowl with the salt and combine with as little boiling water as possible, about 3 Tbsp, to make a dough that is soft but not sticky.

2 Form the dough into balls, roll and flatten them on a lightly floured pastry board to make small pancakes.

3 Heat a pan without fat or oil and cook the chapathis for about 2 minutes on each side, until speckled and puffy.

NOTE
Chapathis can be half cooked, for 1½ minutes on each side, then frozen. The use of boiling water in this recipe ensures that the chapathis will be soft.

(Photograph, see page 131)

YOGURT BREAD
(Puri Dahiwallah)

INGREDIENTS (Makes 12-14)
1½-2 cups all-purpose flour
2-3 Tbsp yogurt
½ tsp salt
oil for frying

1 Sift the flour into a bowl, make a well in the middle, add the yogurt and salt and combine with as little warm water as possible, about 3 Tbsp, to make a dough that is soft but not sticky.

2 Pull off a small piece of dough and roll it into a ball on a lightly floured pastry board, then roll and flatten into a pancake. Repeat with the rest of the dough.

3 Heat about 1 inch of oil in a pan, add the puri and fry for 2 minutes each side, until speckled and puffy.

(Photograph, see page 130)

DAL BREAD
(Dal Puri Roti)

INGREDIENTS (Serves 6-8)
¾-1 cup yellow split peas
4-6 cloves garlic, finely chopped
2 green chili peppers, finely chopped
1 tsp ground cumin
½ tsp turmeric
3 cups all-purpose flour
¼ cup butter or ghee, diced
2 Tbsp oil
½ tsp baking powder
salt

1 Pick over the split peas, wash well and cook in about 3¾ cups water for 10-15 minutes, until the peas can be mashed with the back of a wooden spoon. Drain well.

2 Grind, pound or blend in a blender or food processor the peas, garlic and green chili. Mix the cumin and turmeric with 1 tsp water and blend into the purée, which should be dry rather than loose.

3 Sift the flour into a bowl, make a well in the middle and add the butter or ghee, oil, baking powder and ½ tsp salt. Combine the ingredients to make a dough, adding as little warm water as possible, about 3 Tbsp. The dough should be soft but not sticky.

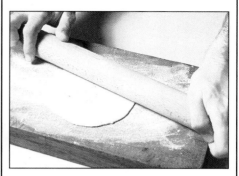

4 Pull off a small piece of dough and roll it into a ball on a lightly floured pastry board. Make a hollow in the ball and stuff in a spoonful of split pea mix. Stretch the dough to cover the stuffing, then roll and flatten the ball to make a small pancake. Repeat with the rest of the dough.

5 Heat a flat pan without any fat or oil. (You can buy a special chapathi pan — a *tava* — but a griddle will do.) Cook the puri in the hot pan for about 2 minutes on each side, until speckled and puffy.

(Photograph, see page 130)

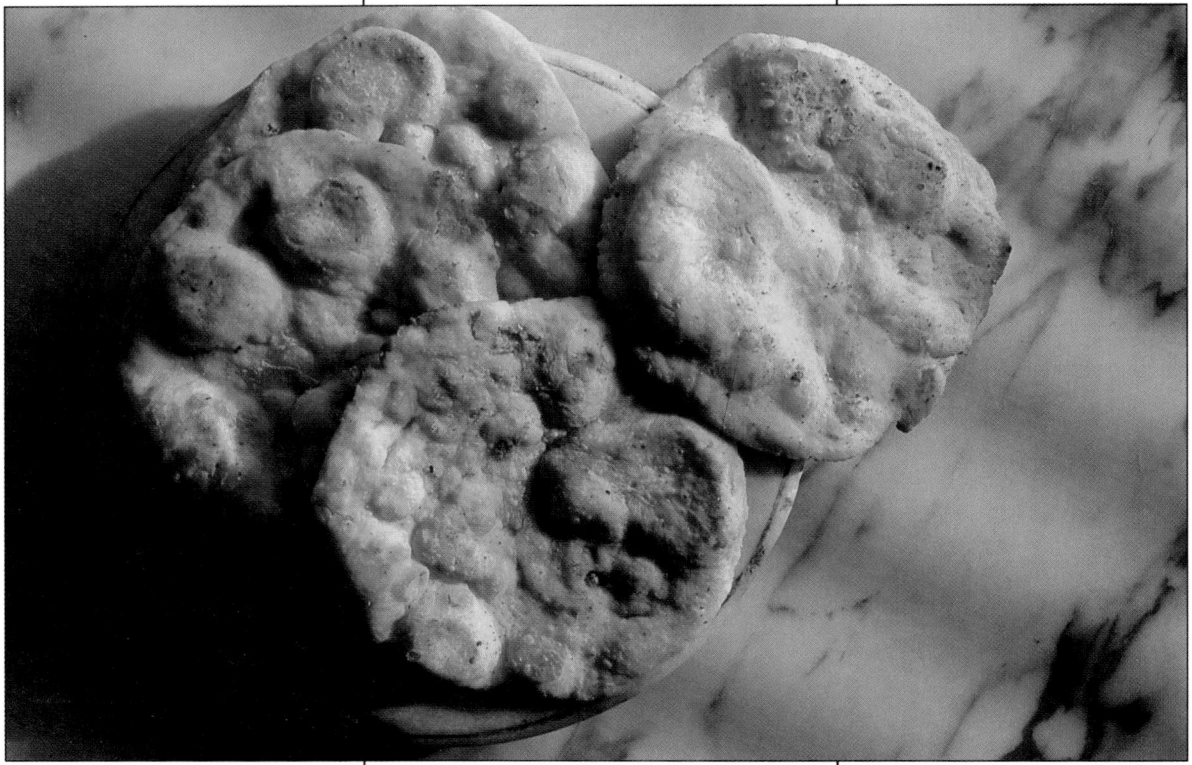

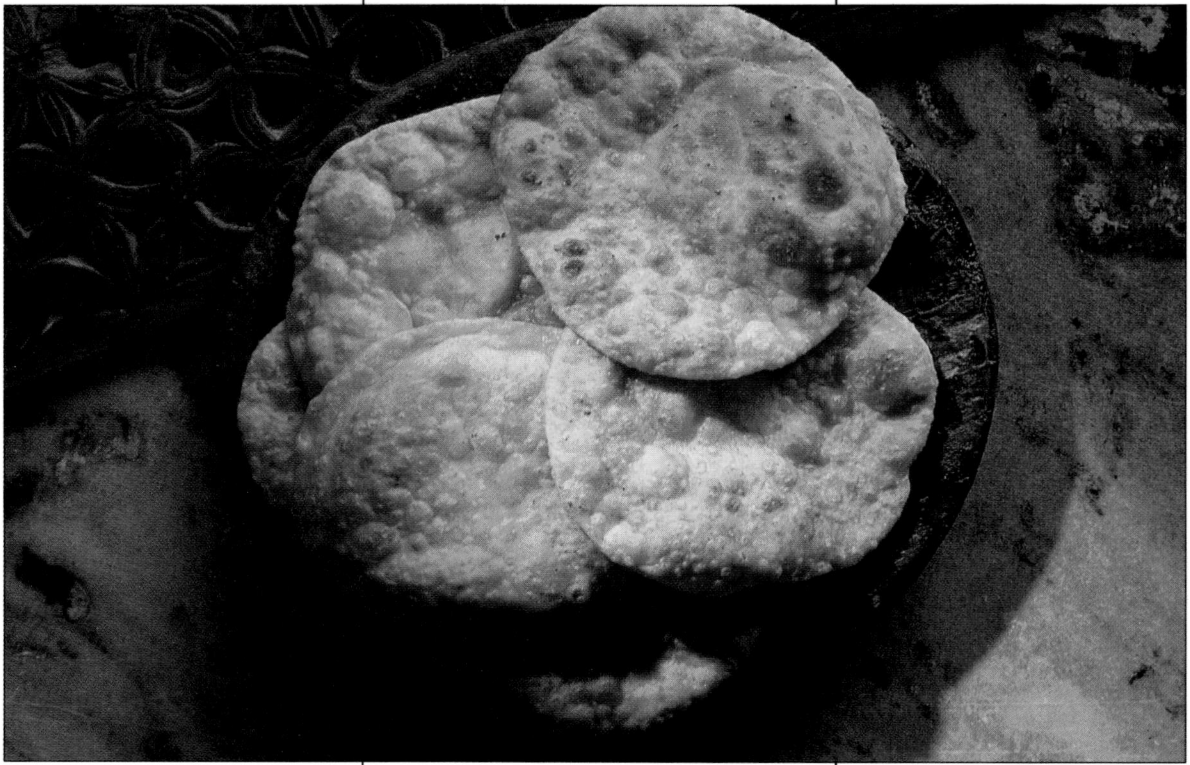

ABOVE Wholewheat Unleavened
Bread
(*Chapathis*)
See page 128

ABOVE OPPOSITE Dal Bread
(*Dal Puri Roti*)
See page 129

BELOW OPPOSITE Yogurt Bread
(*Puri Dahiwallah*)
See page 128

SAVORY RICE
Chawal

Basmati is the best long-grained Indian rice. It is grown in the foothills of the Himalayas and can be aged for up to 15 years to mature its distinctive nutty flavor. If basmati rice is not available, use regular long-grain rice.

When you cook Basmati rice, pick it over first. Measure out the required quantity and pour it onto a tray, go through it removing any bits that are not rice. The next thing is to wash it in two or three changes of cold water and swirl it around until the water looks whitish in color; this is the starch being washed off. Drain and repeat until the water is clear. You may need to wash the rice more than three times.

If you have time, let the rice soak for at least 20 minutes before cooking and then drain very thoroughly. Rice should be cooked in 1½ times its volume of water. You can get the water quantity right by measuring both rice and water in a measuring cup.

Rice is often fried before it its boiled. You will need a heavy, flat-bottomed pot with a tightly fitting lid. Heat some oil in the pot and add the aromatics. Pour in the dry or drained rice and cook gently, stirring, until it is translucent. This means that it has absorbed all the oil it can.

Add the water and bring to a boil, then turn the heat to very low, put on the tightly fitting lid and cook undisturbed for 20 minutes. After this time, stir the rice with a fork, then cover and continue to cook for about five more minutes, or until tender. The grains of rice should be separate.

The cooking process can be finished off in a slow oven to dry the rice if you prefer.

LEMON RICE
(Nimbowala Chawal)

INGREDIENTS (Serves 4)
2-2¼ cups cooked basmati rice
2 Tbsp lemon juice
¼ tsp asafoetida
½ tsp turmeric
salt
2 Tbsp oil
½ tsp mustard seeds
1 tsp polished split black lentils (urid dal)
6 curry leaves
2 Tbsp split gram (chana dal), soaked in
  water for 20 minutes, then drained
1 Tbsp finely grated fresh ginger
1 green chili pepper, chopped

1 Mix the rice with the lemon juice, asafoetida, turmeric and salt to taste.

2 Heat the oil in a pan, add the mustard seeds, dal, curry leaves and split gram and fry until all the mustard seeds have popped.

3 Add the ginger, green chili and rice and heat through, stirring, for about 5 minutes, until hot.

4 Add extra salt to taste.

(Photograph, see page 134)

TOMATO RICE
(Tamatar Chawal)

INGREDIENTS (Serves 4)
2 Tbsp oil
1/2 tsp mustard seeds
2 Tbsp split gram (chana dal), soaked in
    water for 20 minutes, then drained
6 curry leaves
1 red chili pepper, cut into pieces
1 onion, chopped
1 Tbsp finely grated fresh ginger
2 cloves garlic, sliced
1 green chili pepper, chopped
1 1/2 cups peeled and chopped tomatoes
1 tsp sugar
2-2 1/4 cups cooked basmati rice
1 tsp ghee
salt

1 Heat the oil in a pan, add the mustard seeds, split gram, curry leaves and red chili and fry until all the mustard seeds have popped and the gram is golden brown.

2 Add the onion, ginger, garlic and green chili and fry for 3-5 minutes, stirring.

3 Add the tomato and sugar and cook, mashing the tomato with the back of a wooden spoon to make a thick paste.

4 Stir in the rice and ghee and heat through, stirring, for about 5 minutes. Add extra salt to taste.

(Photograph, see page 134)

RICE WITH YOGURT
(Dahi Chawal)

INGREDIENTS (Serves 4)
1 cup yogurt
2-2 1/4 cups cooked basmati rice
2 Tbsp oil
2 tsp polished split black lentils (urid dal)
1 tsp mustard seeds
4-6 curry leaves
2 red or green chili peppers, chopped
salt

1 Mix the yogurt into the rice, without mashing the grains.

2 Heat the oil in a pan, add the lentils and fry until light brown.

3 Add the mustard seeds, curry leaves and chili and fry until all the seeds have popped.

4 Stir the contents of the pan into the rice, mixing carefully, and add salt to taste.

(Photograph, see page 135)

ABOVE Lemon Rice
(Nimbowala Chawal)
See page 132

ABOVE Tomato Rice
(Tamatar Chawal)
See page 133

ABOVE Rice with Yogurt
(Dahi Chawal)
See page 133

CHUTNEYS, SALADS & SNACKS

Accompaniments are served with every meal to give a greater balance of tastes and extra protein and vitamins. They are also eaten as snacks between meals. The streets of India are full of carts selling appetizing delicacies — lentil patties, rice puffs, bread and chutney, roasted chick-peas — intended to inspire hunger in the passersby, who can eat them as they walk along.

There are several types of chutney. Some keep for months and are better after a period of maturing. Some keep for several days in a cool place, and others are made to be eaten immediately. Those cooked with vinegar, sugar and spices keep the longest. Pickles are marinated, rather than cooked. Fruit, vegetables, fish and even meat can be marinated and left to mature for long periods in spiced oils. Other chutneys are made from fresh herbs, such as coriander, and can be eaten immediately.

In Indian homes where dozens of different pickles were made, traditionally they would be left outside in the sun covered in cheesecloth to mature by day and stored in a cool place with the lid on at night. Nowadays many of the chutneys are made in factories and they do not taste quite the same.

Pickles and chutneys can be spicy, sweet, tart, hot, sour, mild or aromatic. The more variety, the better. They are best served with plain foods such as rice and bread, or with lightly spiced dishes. They should not have to compete with the flavor of the dish they accompany, and they should certainly not overwhelm it.

A yogurt relish called *raita* is often served to provide a cooling contrast to a hot, spicy meal, and a refreshing salad of onion, lettuce, tomato and cucumber, dressed with lemon or lime, serves the same purpose.

COCONUT CHUTNEY
(Thankai Chatni)

INGREDIENTS
1⅓ cups finely grated fresh coconut
3 red chili peppers, chopped and seeded
¼ cup yogurt
1 Tbsp oil
½ tsp mustard seeds
4 curry leaves
salt

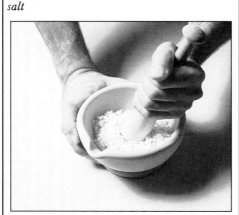

1 Grind, pound or blend in a blender or food processor the coconut and 2 red chili peppers, then stir in the yogurt.

2 Heat the oil in a pan, add the mustard seeds and fry until they have all popped, then add the remaining red chili and the curry leaves and continue to fry for 2-3 minutes.

3 Add to the coconut mixture with salt to taste.

(Photograph, see page 139)

TAMARIND CHUTNEY
(Amli Chatni)

INGREDIENTS
1 Tbsp coriander seeds
1 tsp peppercorns
½ tsp cumin seeds
½ tsp fenugreek seeds
1 tsp mustard seeds
½ tsp asafoetida
5 red chili peppers
2-3 Tbsp oil
1 tsp polished split black lentils (urid dal)
1 tsp split gram (chana dal) soaked for 20
    minutes, then drained
6 curry leaves
¼ cup shelled peanuts
juice from 8oz seedless tamarind
    (see page 19)
2 Tbsp brown sugar
salt
1 Tbsp sesame seeds
⅓-⅔ cups dried unsweetened coconut

1 Heat a skillet without any butter or oil and add the coriander, peppercorns, cumin, fenugreek, half the mustard seeds, half the asafoetida and 4 red chilis. Roast the spices for about 5minutes, shaking the pan to prevent burning. Pound or grind the spices to a fine powder and set aside.

2 Heat the oil in a pan, add the remaining mustard seeds, the lentils, split gram, curry leaves and remaining chili, cut into 3 or 4 pieces, and fry until all the seeds have popped.

3 Add the peanuts and fry for a further 3 or 4 minutes, then add the tamarind juice, the roasted spice powder, sugar, ½ tsp salt and remaining asafoetida.

4 Heat another pan without fat or oil, roast the sesame seeds and coconut and add to the chutney. Stir well, adding extra salt to taste.

(Photograph, see page 138)

GREEN CORIANDER CHUTNEY
(Hari Daniya Chatni)

INGREDIENTS
leaves from 3-4 sprigs coriander
1 or 2 green chili peppers
1 Tbsp grated fresh ginger
salt
2 Tbsp lemon juice
½ tsp sugar

1 Grind, pound or blend in a blender or food processor the coriander leaves, green chili, ginger and ½ tsp salt to make a thick paste.

2 Stir in the lemon juice and add sugar and extra salt to taste.

(Photograph, see page 138)

LEFT Tamarind Chutney
(Amli Chatni)
See page 137

BELOW Green Coriander Chutney
(Hari Daniya Chatni)
See page 137

OPPOSITE Coconut Chutney
(Thankai Chatni)
See page 136

GREEN MANGO CHUTNEY
(Aam Chatni)

INGREDIENTS
8oz hard green mango
²⁄₃ cup finely grated fresh coconut
1 red chili pepper or 1 tsp chili powder
1 tsp mustard seeds
1 Tbsp yogurt
1 Tbsp oil
4 curry leaves
salt

1 Chop the mango as finely as possible, with or without the skin. Place in a bowl.

2 Grind, pound or blend in a blender or food processor the coconut, chili pepper and half the mustard seeds, add to the mango and stir in the yogurt.

3 Heat the oil in a pan, add the remaining mustard seeds and the curry leaves and fry until all the seeds have popped, then stir into the chutney. Add salt to taste.

(Photograph, see page 142)

PEANUT SOYA SAUCE
(Seng Dana Chatni)

INGREDIENTS
²⁄₃ cup shelled peanuts, skinned
2 red chili peppers, cut into 3 or 4 pieces
½ tsp salt
2 Tbsp soy sauce
1 Tbsp lemon juice
1 Tbsp brown sugar
2 Tbsp oil

1 Pound, grind or blend the first 6 ingredients.

2 Heat the oil in a saucepan, add the peanut mixture and cook until it begins to bubble. Remove from the heat and stir well.

(Photograph, see page 142)

BLACK LENTIL CHUTNEY
(Urid Dal Chatni)

INGREDIENTS
½ cup polished split black lentils (urid dal)
1 or 2 red chili peppers
¼ tsp asafoetida
⅔ cup finely grated fresh coconut
juice from 1 Tbsp seedless tamarind
*   (see page 19)*
salt

1 Pick over the lentils. Heat a pan without fat or oil, add the lentils, 1 chili and the asafoetida and cook, shaking the pan to prevent burning, until the lentils are golden.

2 Pound the roasted spices together.

3 Grind, pound or blend in a blender or food processor the coconut and tamarind with 1-2 Tbsp water, then add the roasted spice powder and grind them together, adding a little more water if necessary.

4 Add salt to taste.

(Photograph, see page 142)

YOGURT AND TOMATO RELISH
(Tamatar Raita)

INGREDIENTS
½ cup tomatoes, diced
1 small onion, finely chopped
½ cup yogurt
leaves from 1 sprig of coriander
1 green chili pepper, finely chopped
1 Tbsp finely grated fresh ginger
½ tsp salt
½ tsp ground cumin, roasted without fat

1 Mix the tomato with the onion in a bowl. You can reduce the strength of the onion by rinsing it in hot water, if desired.

2 Mix the yogurt in another bowl. Stir the dressing into the vegetables and add extra salt to taste.

(Photograph, see page 143)

ABOVE **Green Mango Chutney**
(Aam Chatni)
See page 140

ABOVE **Black Lentil Chutney**
(Urid Dal Chatni)
See page 141

ABOVE **Peanut Soya Sauce**
(Seng Dana Chatni)
See page140

ABOVE Yogurt and Tomato Relish
(Tamatar Raita)
See page 141

SWEET TOMATO CHUTNEY
(Tamatar Ki Chatni)

INGREDIENTS
1lb tomatoes
¼ cup sugar
½ tsp ground cardamom seeds
3 cloves
½ tsp chili powder
1 Tbsp oil
½ tsp mustard seeds
1 Tbsp white wine vinegar
salt
4 curry leaves

1 Immerse the tomatoes in a bowl of boiling water for about 2 minutes, until the skins split. Drain them, allow to cool, peel and chop.

2 Bring ⅔ cup water to a boil in a small pan, add the sugar and tomato and cook for 5 minutes, stirring.

3 Add the cardamom, cloves and chili powder and continue cooking, mashing the tomato with the back of a wooden spoon to make a thick paste. Remove the pan from the heat.

4 Heat the oil in a pan, add the mustard seeds and fry until they have all popped, then add to the tomato.

5 Stir in the vinegar, add salt to taste and sprinkle with the curry leaves.

(Photograph, see page 146)

TOMATO SALAD
(Kachumbar)

INGREDIENTS (Serves 4)
1lb tomatoes, sliced
2 green chili peppers, finely sliced
2 tsp sugar
1 Tbsp lemon juice
leaves from 1 or 2 sprigs of coriander
salt

1 Mix the tomato with the chili.

2 Sprinkle with sugar, lemon juice and coriander leaves. Mix well and add salt to taste.

(Photograph, see page 146)

CABBAGE FRITTERS
(Gobi Pakoras)

INGREDIENTS (Serves 4)
1 cup chick-pea flour (besan)
1 ¼ cup grated hard white cabbage
1 small onion, finely sliced
2 green chili peppers, thinly sliced
1 Tbsp finely grated fresh ginger
4-6 curry leaves, chopped
1 tsp salt
½ tsp chili powder
½ tsp garam masala (see page 17)
oil for deep frying

1 Mix the flour with ⅔ cup water in a bowl to make a batter.

2 Add all the ingredients except the oil and stir well to coat.

3 Heat a quantity of oil for deep frying, add the cabbage in batter by the tablespoonful and fry until golden. Drain on paper towels.

4 Serve with chutney.

(Photograph, see page 147)

CHICKEN AND VEGETABLE SALAD
(Murghi aur Kachumbar)

INGREDIENTS (Serves 4-6)
1⅓ cups cooked chicken, cut into manageable
*   pieces*
1 or 2 apples, cored and cut into wedges
1 cup shredded white cabbage
2 tomatoes, cut into eighths
1 green chili pepper, finely chopped
½ tsp ground pepper
¼ tsp ground nutmeg
salt
2 Tbsp lemon juice
leaves from 1 or 2 sprigs coriander

1 Mix the chicken with the apple, cabbage, tomato and green chili.

2 Sprinkle on the pepper, nutmeg and salt.

3 Squeeze the lemon juice over and toss the salad. Decorate with coriander leaves.

(Photograph, see page 147)

MELON WITH ORANGE JUICE
(Tarbuch aur Mosamki Ka Rus)

INGREDIENTS (Serves 4)
1 honeydew melon
1 Tbsp butter or ghee
½ tsp ground cumin
juice of 2 sweet oranges
1 Tbsp lemon juice
2 Tbsp sugar

1 Cut melon into wedges, remove the pith, seeds and skin. Cut the flesh into cubes. Place in a bowl.

2 Heat the butter or ghee in a saucepan, add the cumin and let it sizzle until the fragrance emerges.

3 Meanwhile, mix the orange and lemon juices with the sugar and 1 Tbsp water.

4 Sprinkle the syrup over the melon, add the cumin and serve.

(Photograph, see page 146)

LEFT Sweet Tomato Chutney
(Tamatar Ki Chatni)
See page 144

ABOVE Tomato Salad
(Kachumbar)
See page 144

ABOVE Melon with Orange Juice
(Tarbuch aur Mosamki Ka Rus)
See page 145

ABOVE Chicken and Vegetable
Salad
(Murghi aur Kachumbar)
See page 145

ABOVE Cabbage Fritters
(Gobi Pakoras)
See page 144

DESSERTS
Mithi

The simplest and one of the best ways of ending an Indian meal is with fresh fruit. In India this might be mangoes, guavas, jackfruit, pineapple, melon, cherries, oranges, apples or bananas. The Alphonso mango from Maharashtra in the west is considered the best of all. Most of these fruits should be readily available from any good grocery store.

A mango is ripe if it gives a little when pressed. An unripe mango can be ripened at home in a warm place, wrapped in paper. You can then chill it, peel it and serve it sliced, with or without cream. Do not throw the pit away without nibbling off the rest of the flesh.

Desserts and sweets are served on special occasions, such as weddings. Many of them are made with fruit, nuts, spices and milk. Coconut is a natural ingredient for a sweet dish, but more surprising is the imaginative use of vegetables for desserts. In this section you will find halvahs made from pumpkin and beet. They look spectacular and taste absolutely delicious.

All the desserts here can be made quite easily at home, but there are many more elaborate Indian confections that are best left to the experts, who are nothing if not ingenious. Indian kulfilwallahs (ice cream sellers) made ice cream long before there were freezers. They put the mixture into metal cones in a large churn made of clay, which was filled with pebbles, saltpeter and other natural substances and rocked until the ice cream froze.

PINEAPPLE PUDDING
(Ananas Pudding)

INGREDIENTS (Serves 2)
1¼ cups canned pineapple chunks, drained
2 eggs
⅔ cup milk
½ cup sugar
¼ tsp ground cinnamon
3 cloves

1 Arrange the pineapple pieces in a greased ovenproof dish.

2 Beat the eggs with the milk and sugar and pour over the pineapple, then sprinkle on the cinnamon and cloves.

3 Set the dish in a roasting pan of boiling water and bake in a preheated 325°F oven for about 45 minutes until lightly set.

(Photograph, see page 150)

MANGO SOUFFLE
(*Aam Pudding*)

INGREDIENTS (Serves 4)
4 eggs
2 tsp unflavoured gelatin
1¼ cups mango juice or 8oz mango pulp
2 Tbsp granulated sugar
salt
2 Tbsp superfine sugar
½ tsp vanilla extract

1 Separate the eggs, placing the yolks in a heatproof mixing bowl.

2 In a small bowl, sprinkle the gelatin over 3 Tbsp water and let stand until softened.

3 Beat the yolks well and mix with the mango juice or pulp.

4 Stir in the granulated sugar, gelatin and ½ tsp salt.

5 Place the bowl over a pan of simmering water, taking care that the bowl does not touch the water or the eggs will scramble. Beat the mixture for 10 minutes, then take off the heat.

6 Whisk the egg whites with ½ tsp salt and the superfine sugar until stiff, then fold into the yolks, adding the vanilla extract.

7 Divide the mixture among 4 small dishes and chill before serving.
(*Photograph, see page 151*)

BEET HALVAH
(*Chukander Italva*)

INGREDIENTS (Serves 4)
1lb beets
2½ cups milk
¾ cup sugar
½ cup ghee
¼ tsp ground cardamom seeds
10 almonds, chopped

1 Scrape the skin from the beets, then grate coarsely.

2 Put the beets in a pan with the milk and sugar and cook gently for 30 minutes or more, stirring briskly, until all the milk has evaporated.

3 Add the ghee, cardamom and almonds and continue cooking, stirring constantly, until the mixture is thick and sticky.

4 Spread the mixture about 2 inches deep in a greased dish with straight sides.

5 Let stand for about 45 minutes to set, then cut into squares.

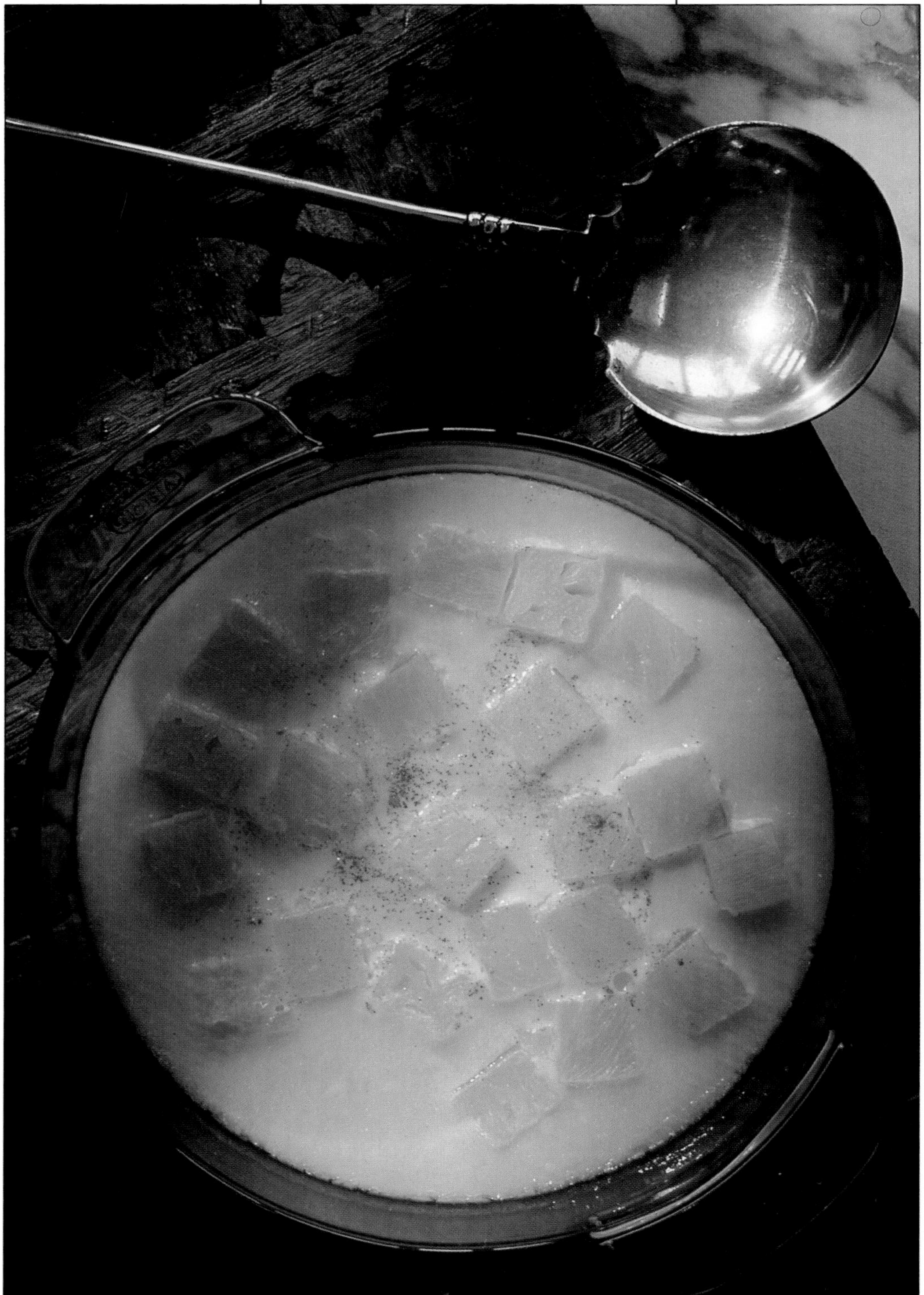

ABOVE Mango Soufflé
(Aam Pudding)
See page 149

OPPOSITE Pineapple Pudding
(Ananas Pudding)
See page 148

PUMPKIN HALVAH
(Pethi Halva)

INGREDIENTS (Serves 4)
1lb pumpkin, preferably white (see page 40)
2½ cups milk
⅔ cup sugar
1 tsp rosewater
½ cup ghee or butter
¼ tsp ground cardamom seeds
10-15 cashew nuts, halved

1 Scrape the seeds and strings from the inside of the pumpkin, cut the flesh from the skin and chop into chunks.

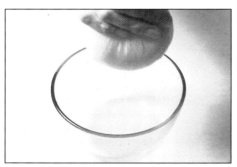

2 Grate the pumpkin coarsely, put in a square of cheesecloth and squeeze out all the moisture.

3 Combine the pumpkin in a pan with the milk, sugar and rosewater and cook over low heat for 30 minutes or more, stirring briskly, until all the milk has evaporated.

4 Stir in the ghee and continue cooking until it separates. Drain off any butter not absorbed by the pumpkin mixture.

5 Stir in the cardamom and cashew nuts and spread the mixture about two inches deep in a greased dish with straight sides.

6 Let stand for about 45 minutes, until set, then cut into squares.

(Photograph, see page 154)

PLANTAIN JAGGERY
(*Kela Gur*)

INGREDIENTS (Serves 4)
4 ripe plantains, unpeeled
1 cup jaggery (raw sugar; use brown sugar
if jaggery is not available)

1 Cut the plantains into 2 inch lengths, place in a pan and add just enough water to cover.

2 Add the jaggery and cook for 35–40 minutes, until all the water has evaporated.

3 Allow to cool, peel, then chill and serve cold.

(Photograph, see page 155)

STEAMED PLANTAIN CAKE
(*Kela Cake*)

INGREDIENTS (Serves 4)
1½-2 cups self-rising flour
1 Tbsp melted ghee
3 or 4 ripe plantains, peeled and thinly sliced
⅔ cup finely grated coconut
1 cup brown sugar
½ tsp ground cardamom seeds

1 Sift the flour into a bowl, make a well in the middle and pour in the melted ghee. Gradually adding as little warm water as possible (about 6 Tbsp), work the ingredients into a smooth dough.

2 Mix the plantains with the remaining ingredients.

3 Cut aluminum foil into four 9 inch squares and divide the dough among them. With your finger or a spoon, dipped in water to prevent sticking, spread the dough out to within 1 inch of each edge of the foil.

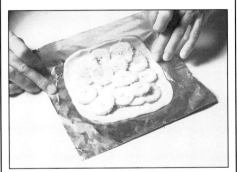

4 Divide the plantain mixture among the sheets of dough and spread to cover.

5 Fold each foil sheet over in the middle and fold over the edges, pressing down well to seal.

6 Put the foil packets in a steamer over a pan of boiling water and steam, covered, for 25-30 minutes, making sure that the foil does not touch the water.

(Photograph, see page 155)

ABOVE Pumpkin Halvah
(Pethi Halva)
See page 152

ABOVE OPPOSITE Plantain Jaggery
(Kela Gur)
See page 153

BELOW OPPOSITE Steamed Plantain
Cake
(Kela Cake)
See page 153

Glossary

Adrak Fresh ginger (see below).
Amchur Dried mango powder. Has a bittersweet flavor.
Amli Tamarind (see below).
Asafoetida A truffle-flavored brown resin, available in powdered or lump form, and often used in cooking with beans. If you buy the lump form, crumble off a small piece and crush it between two sheets of paper.
Atta Wholewheat flour. Wheat is often ground at home in India and used to make unleavened flat breads.
Basmati rice The finest Indian long-grained rice, grown in the foothills of the Himalayas.
Besan Also known as chick-pea flour, this is the flour made from chick-peas. It is used particularly in the south for making pancakes and steamed patties.
Biriyani A rice and vegetable, meat or seafood oven-cooked dish.
Cardamom Both black and green cardamoms are available, although the black ones are not often available. They are large and hairy. Use the green ones for the recipes in this book.
Chana dal A very versatile dried split pea. It looks like the ordinary yellow split pea, but is smaller with a sweeter, nuttier flavor. It can be cooked until soft for the dish called simply "dal", or, as in southern India, it can be used as a spice.
Chawal Rice.
Chick-peas Also called **garbanzo beans.** As they demand hours of cooking before they become tender, it is often cheaper to buy the canned variety.
Chili peppers Can be brought fresh, in which case they are normally green, or dried, in which case they are red. Chili peppers are very hot and should be handled with care and used according to taste.
Cinnamon Can be bought powdered or, better, in sticks. These sticks are the rolled bark of the cinnamon tree and have a warm, spicy flavor.
Coconut Characteristic of the cooking of southern India. Buy a fresh coconut to

extract the milk (see page 19) or use dried unsweetened coconut to thicken sauces or garnish finished dishes. Dried unsweetened coconut can be bought in Asian and Indian markets as well as in healthfood stores.
Coriander Also known as **cilantro** or Chinese parsley. Both the seeds and leaves of this plant are used. It can be grown as easily as parsley. The seeds are small and round, and are used either whole or ground. The leaves are bright green and have a strong, bittersweet flavor.
Cumin seeds White or black, these seeds can be used whole or ground.
Curry leaves Can sometimes be bought fresh, which is preferable to using them dried. Used extensively in the south of India, they are mainly added to food just before it is served.
Dahi Yogurt.
Dalchini Cinnamon (see above).
Dals Dried split peas, usually bought skinned.
Dhaniya Coriander (see above).
Elaichi Cardamom (see above).
Fenugreek seeds Chunky, tawny-colored seeds, often used roasted and ground. They have a bitter taste.
Fenugreek leaves are a vegetable used like spinach, to which the plant is related.
Garam masala A mixture of spices ground together (see page 21), it is sprinkled on some dishes after they have been cooked.
Ghee Clarified butter. It can be made at home (see page 22) and does not need to be refrigerated.
Ginger Fresh ginger *(adrak)* is a fawn-colored rhizome. Ginger can also be bought powdered *(soondth).*
Gosht Meat. Goat is the meat most often eaten in India.
Gram flour Made from chick-peas and also known as *besan.*
Haldi Turmeric (see below).
Halvah A sweet dish.
Hara Green.

Hing Asafoetida (see above).
Jaggery Raw sugar, eaten as is and used to flavor various dishes, even vegetable curries.
Jeera Cumin *(see above).*
Jingha Shrimp or langoustine.
Kofta Meat or banana balls.
Lassi A yogurt drink (see page 13).
Luong Cloves.
Machi Fish.
Masala Spices.
Masoor dal Skinned split red lentils.
Moong dal Skinned split mung beans.
Murghi Chicken.
Mustard oil A yellow oil made from mustard seeds that is pungent when raw and sweet when heated. Much used in Kashmir and Bengal.
Mustard seeds Small yellow or black seeds often popped in hot oil, giving them a nutty, sweet flavor. When ground for mustard powder their character is quite different — hot and smarting.
Nariel Coconut (see above).
Neem Curry leaves (see above).
Papaya A fruit with good digestive properties.
Pilaf Fried rice dish.
Raita A cooling side dish made with yogurt.
Roti Bread.
Sambar powder A Southern Indian spice mix for vegetable curries (see page 22).
Soondth Powdered ginger (see above).
Tamarind The bean-like fruit of the tamarind tree, much used in southern Indian cooking.
Tava A flat cast-iron pan used for making bread.
Thali A large tray, often of wrought metal.
Toor dal A glossy dark yellow split pea.
Toran A style of cooking where the dish remains dry.
Urid dal Polished split black lentils, often used as a spice in southern India.
Vark Silver and gold leaf used to decorate food on special occasions. It is edible.
Vindaloo A high spiced and hot curry, traditionally from Goa.

Index

Specialist Suppliers

California
Bezjian Groceries
4725 Santa Monica Boulevard
Los Angeles, California 94702
Tel: (415) 548-4110

India Gifts and Food
643 Post Street,
San Francisco, California 94109
Tel: (415) 771-5041

District of Columbia
Spices and Foods, Unlimited, Inc.
2018A Florida Avenue NW
Washington D.C. 20009
Tel: (202) 265-1909

Illinois
India Groceries
5010 North Sheridan Road
Chicago, Illinois 60640
Tel: (312) 334-3351

Maryland
Indian Sub-Continental Store
908 Philadelphia Avenue
Silver Spring, Maryland 20910
Tel: (301) 589-8417

Michigan
India Foods and Boutique
37-29 Cass Avenue
Detroit, Michigan 48201
Tel: (313) 831-0056

New Jersey
Bombay Bazaar
797 Newark Avenue
Jersey City, New Jersey 07306
Tel: (201) 963-5907

Krishna Grocery Store
103 Broadway
Passaic, New Jersey 07057
Tel: (201) 472-3025

New York
Annapurna
127 East 28 Street
New York, New York 10016
Tel: (202) 889-7540

Foods of India
120 Lexington Avenue,
New York, New York 10016
Tel: (212) 683-4419

House of Spices
76-77 Broadway
Jackson Heights, New York 11373
Tel: (212) 476-1577

Kalpana Indian Groceries and Spices, Inc.
42-75 Main Street
Flushing, New York 11355
Tel: (212) 961-4111

Maharaj Bazar
665 Flatbush Avenue
Brooklyn, New York 11225
Tel: (212) 941-2666

Sahadi Importing Company, Inc.
187 Atlantic Avenue
Brooklyn, New York 11201
Tel: (212) 624-4550

Oregon
Porter's Foods Unlimited
125 West 11th Avenue
Eugene, Oregon 97401
Tel: (503) 342-3629

Pennsylvania
House of Spices of New York
4101 Walnut Street
West Philadelphia,
Pennsylvania 19104
Tel: (215) 222-1111

India Bazaar
3358 Fifth Avenue
Pittsburgh, Pennsylvania 15213
Tel: (412) 682-1172

Texas
Jay Store
4023 West Himier Street
Houston, Texas 77027
Tel: (713) 871-9270

Yoga and Health Center
2912 Oaklawn Avenue
Dallas, Texas 75219
Tel: (214) 528-8681

Washington
Specialty Spice House
Pike Place Market
Seattle, Washington 98105
Tel: (206) 622-6340

Specialty Spice House
Tacoma Mall
Tacoma, Washington 98049
Tel: (206) 474-7524

Canada
S. Enkin, Inc.
1203 St. Lawrence
Montreal, Quebec H2X 2S6
Tel: (514) 886-3202

Kalpana Indian Groceries and Spices, Inc.
1763 Danforth Avenue
Toronto, Ontario M4C IJ1
Tel: (416) 698-9882